Short and Simple Guide to Life Insurance

Short and Simple Guide to Life Insurance

Alan Lavine
and
Gail Liberman

Authors Choice Press
San Jose New York Lincoln Shanghai

Short and Simple Guide to Life Insurance

Authors Choice Press
an imprint of iUniverse.com, Inc.

For information address:
iUniverse.com, Inc.
620 North 48th Street, Suite 201
Lincoln, NE 68504-3467
www.iuniverse.com

Originally published by John Wiley

ISBN: 0-595-14448-9

Printed in the United States of America

Contents

1

Understanding and Using Life Insurance

Most American families have life insurance protection. Unfortunately, many people buy the wrong type or amount of coverage. So they drop their life insurance policy within 10 years after the purchase.

Many people don't like to think or talk about life insurance. Death is a difficult topic to discuss. Nevertheless, next to buying a house and saving for retirement, the purchase of life insurance is one of the most important financial decisions anyone makes. That probably is why statistics show that most people buy life insurance at some time in their lives. Eight out of ten American families have some life insurance coverage. The average family has $115,000 of coverage according to the American Council of Life Insurance, a trade group in Washington, DC. In 1992, consumers took out $156 billion in insurance coverage. Despite all that protection, the National Insurance Consumers Organization, Alexandria, VA, reports that 20 percent of all policies are dropped after 2 years and almost 50 percent of all policies are cashed out after 10 years.

The lesson to be learned: You won't be one of those who drop their policies if you take the time to learn how life insurance works, how much and what kind you need, and where to get what you want.

You generally don't learn about life insurance in high school or college. Most people only remember fragments of conversations between their parents and a life insurance agent as they sat around the kitchen table.

Unfortunately, that kind of information is not enough. There are many kinds of insurance policies designed to meet people's different psychological and financial needs. Why should you consider paying fat premiums to an insurance company? This is the reason: If you die, your family will be free of at least some of the financial problems the loss of your income would cause. You could probably save $100,000 in a side fund over 25 years by salting away $2,000 a year in a mutual fund that grows at an annual rate of 10 percent. If you do that, though, you have to wait 25 years for the cash. The money won't be available if you die in year 7. Death benefits can be used to cover the policyholder's outstanding debts such as a home mortgage or to pay for a child's college education or to pay estate taxes (as Malcom Forbes did).

WHO BUYS LIFE INSURANCE?

Most people own life insurance to meet the future needs of dependents such as a spouse, a child, or an elderly parent. Some people purchase life insurance for the added purpose of building up cash reserves for future needs, such as retirement or college tuition expenses.

Life insurance is an essential part of financial planning for many of us. Congress has recognized this by according special income tax status to the proceeds from life insurance policies. Death benefits are not taxed. Neither is the interest earnings on the savings portion of a whole life policy. That's what has made cash value life insurance a popular product.

Life insurance is owned by 82 percent of all American households. The average amount of life insurance per insured household was $115,000 by year-end 1989. But the average size policy for each insured person was $35,000 by year-end 1989, according to the American Council of Life Insurance.

In the past, most life insurance purchases were made by men to protect the income needs of their families. Today, women are a more significant part of the life insurance market. A growing number of women are heads of households who purchase life insurance to protect their families. In addition, the growth of two wage-earner families over the past 20 years makes it more important for husbands and wives to properly evaluate their insurance needs and obtain adequate coverage.

According to a 1989 American Council of Life Insurance survey, 65 percent of all women have life insurance coverage. Of those with coverage, 47 percent have individual policies. The remainder have coverage from their employer.

Three out of four men have life insurance; 56 percent have individual coverage, and 44 percent get coverage from the workplace.

The average amount of coverage for married couples with their own life insurance is $78,700.

ACTION ITEM

Seek professional help before you buy life insurance. Insurance and financial planning professionals evaluate your personal finances to determine your present and future insurance needs.

HOW LIFE INSURANCE WORKS: THE RISK FACTOR

Insurance companies can afford to pay out hundreds of millions of dollars each year in death benefits because they are playing a numbers game. Based on historical data, the company knows that only a small percentage of people of a certain age will die in a given year. The insurance company does not know how long a particular person will live, but they do know the average life span of any given group of people of a certain age, income, and state of health. The company can predict the cost to each person in the pool. The mortality table gives the insurance company an idea what it will cost them to pay death benefits each year. Because only a small number may die in a given year or years, the insurance company takes in many more dollars in premiums over the years than they pay out in death benefits in any one year.

Look at it this way: Harry paid $1,000—or one year's premium for a $100,000 insurance policy. The insurance company sold similar policies to 50,000 people. Harry died within a year. His widow collected the $100,000 death benefit.

Did the insurance company lose? No way. The 50,000 people in the insurance pool paid $50 million in premiums—a rather large kitty. Certainly, it is enough to cover the $100,000 paid to Harry's widow.

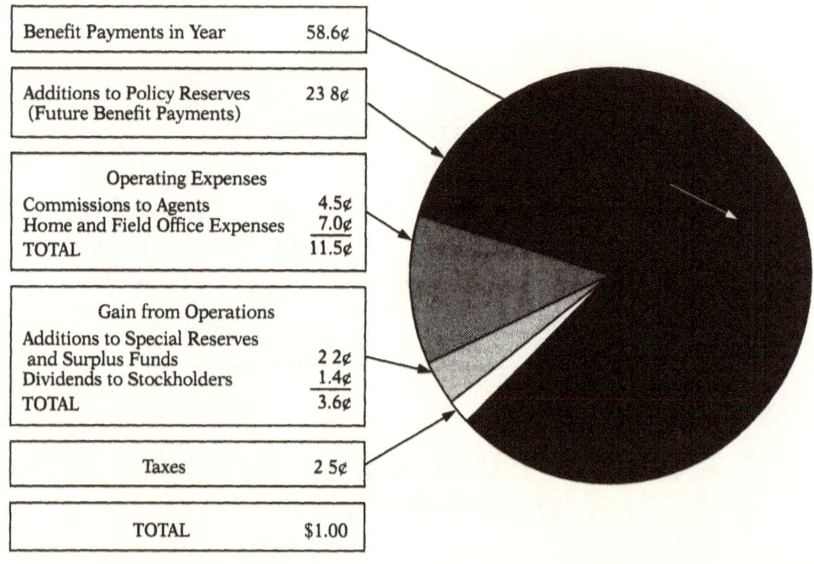

(Source: American Council of Life Insurance, 10/92.)

Figure 1–1

Where your life insurance dollar goes (U.S. Life Insurance Companies, 1991).

Here's another way to look at the situation. You pay a premium for a traditional life insurance policy. The insurance company divides that premium into three parts: Part 1 of the premium buys insurance for you. Part 2 of your money pays the company's business expenses, such as overhead, wages, and sales commissions. Part 3 is invested in a savings or cash value account. Figure 1–1 shows how each dollar's worth of insurance is spent. Figure 1–2 shows how insurance companies invest their assets.

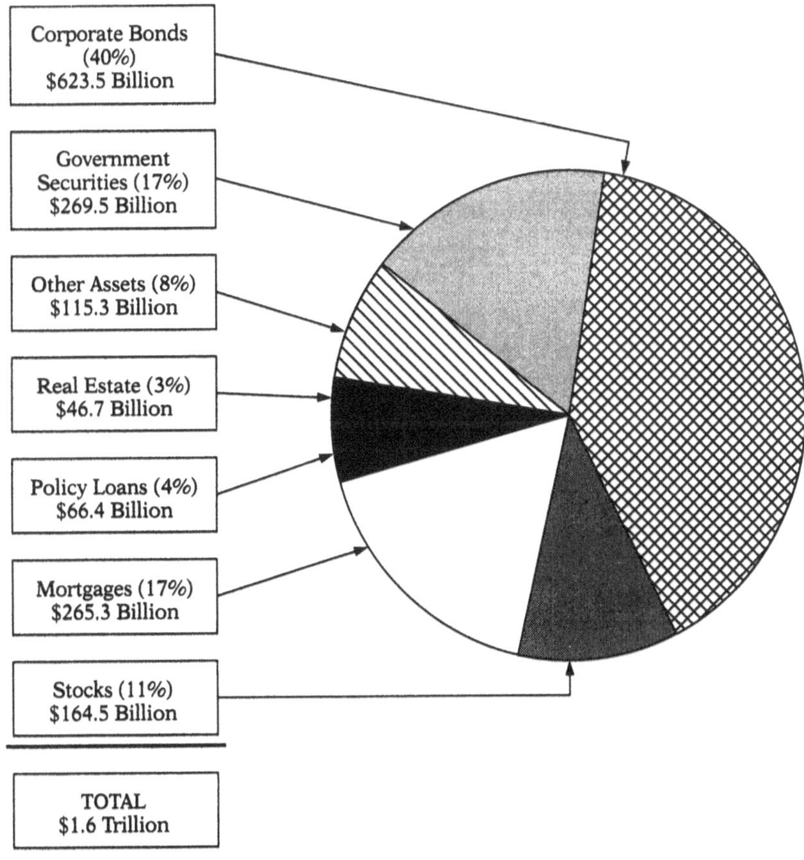

(Source: American Council of Life Insurance, 10/92.)

Figure 1–2

How U.S. life insurance companies invest their assets (1991).

ASSESSING THE RISK

Here's how risk is assessed: You know that if you flip a coin you have a 50-50 chance of it coming up heads or tails. That's a probability of 50 percent. The insurance company knows the probability of people's death based on their age. With a coin, the odds of being right are one out of two. It's different for people. For example, based on the 1980 U.S. Commissioners' standard Ordinary Mortality Table (the one most insurance companies use), the death rate for 45-year-old men is .00455 (see Table 1–1). That means that 445 forty-five-year-old men out of 100,000 will die in any one year. In dollar terms, this means that the insurance company must charge you $4.45 per $1,000 of insurance to cover the cost of death in a given year. That rate is known as a mortality fee. The older you are, the higher the mortality charge.

Table 1–1
Mortality Tables

	Commissioners 1980 Standard Ordinary (1970–1975)			
	Male		***Female***	
Age	***Deaths per 1,000***	***Expectation of Life (Years)***	***Deaths per 1,000***	***Expectation of Life (Years)***
0	4.18	70.83	2.89	75.83
1	1.07	70.13	.87	75.04
2	.99	69.20	.81	74.11
3	.98	68.27	.79	73.17
4	.95	67.34	.77	72.23
5	.90	66.40	.76	71.28
6	.86	65.46	.73	70.34
7	.80	64.52	.72	69.39
8	.76	63.57	.70	68.44
9	.74	62.62	.69	67.48
10	.73	61.66	.68	66.53

Source: American Council of Life Insurance.

Table 1–1 *(Continued)*

	Commissioners 1980 Standard Ordinary (1970–1975)			
	Male		*Female*	
Age	*Deaths per 1,000*	*Expectation of Life (Years)*	*Deaths per 1,000*	*Expectation of Life (Years)*
11	.77	60.71	.69	65.58
12	.85	59.75	.72	64.62
13	.99	58.80	.75	63.67
14	1.15	57.86	.80	62.71
15	1.33	56.93	.85	61.76
16	1.51	56.00	.90	60.82
17	1.67	55.09	.95	59.87
18	1.78	54.18	.98	58.93
19	1.86	53.27	1.02	57.98
20	1.90	52.37	1.05	57.04
21	1.91	51.47	1.07	56.10
22	1.89	50.57	1.09	55.16
23	1.86	49.66	1.11	54.22
24	1.82	48.75	1.14	53.28
25	1.77	47.84	1.16	52.34
26	1.73	46.93	1.19	51.40
27	1.71	46.01	1.22	50.46
28	1.70	45.09	1.26	49.52
29	1.71	44.16	1.30	48.59
30	1.73	43.24	1.35	47.65
31	1.78	42.31	1.40	46.71
32	1.83	41.38	1.45	45.78
33	1.91	40.46	1.50	44.84
34	2.00	39.54	1.58	43.91
35	2.11	38.61	1.65	42.98
36	2.24	37.69	1.76	42.05
37	2.40	36.78	1.89	41.12
38	2.58	35.87	2.04	40.20
39	2.79	34.96	2.22	39.28
40	3.02	34.05	2.42	38.36
41	3.29	33.16	2.64	37.46
42	3.56	32.26	2.87	35.55
43	3.87	31.38	3.09	35.66

Table 1–1 *(Continued)*

	Commissioners 1980 Standard Ordinary (1970–1975)			
	Male		*Female*	
Age	*Deaths per 1,000*	*Expectation of Life (Years)*	*Deaths per 1,000*	*Expectation of Life (Years)*
44	4.19	30.50	3.32	34.77
45	4.55	29.62	3.56	33.88
46	5.92	28.76	3.80	33.00
47	5.32	27.90	4.05	32.12
48	5.74	27.04	4.33	31.25
49	6.21	26.20	4.63	30.39
50	6.71	25.36	4.96	29.53
51	7.30	24.52	5.31	28.67
52	7.96	23.70	5.70	27.82
53	8.71	22.89	6.15	26.98
54	9.56	22.08	6.61	26.14
55	10.47	21.29	7.09	25.31
56	11.46	20.51	7.57	24.49
57	12.49	19.74	8.03	23.67
58	13.59	18.99	8.47	22.86
59	14.77	18.24	8.94	22.05
60	16.08	17.51	9.47	21.25
61	17.54	16.79	10.13	20.44
62	19.19	16.08	10.96	19.65
63	21.06	15.38	12.02	18.86
64	23.14	14.70	13.25	18.08
65	25.42	14.04	14.59	17.32
66	27.85	13.39	16.00	16.57
67	30.44	12.76	17.43	15.83
68	33.19	12.14	18.84	15.10
69	36.17	11.54	20.36	14.38
70	39.51	10.96	22.11	13.67
71	43.30	10.39	24.23	12.97
72	47.65	9.84	26.89	12.28
73	52.64	9.30	30.11	11.60
74	58.19	8.79	33.93	10.95
75	64.19	8.31	38.24	10.32
76	70.53	7.84	42.97	9.71

Table 1–1 *(Continued)*

	Commissioners 1980 Standard Ordinary (1970–1975)			
	Male		*Female*	
Age	*Deaths per 1,000*	*Expectation of Life (Years)*	*Deaths per 1,000*	*Expectation of Life (Years)*
77	77.12	7.40	48.04	9.12
78	83.90	6.97	53.45	8.55
79	91.05	6.57	59.35	8.01
80	98.84	6.18	65.99	7.48
81	107.48	5.80	73.60	6.98
82	227.25	5.44	82.40	6.49
83	128.26	5.09	92.53	6.03
84	140.25	4.77	103.81	5.59
85	152.95	4.46	116.10	5.18
86	166.09	4.18	129.29	4.80
87	279.55	3.91	143.32	4.43
88	193.27	3.66	158.18	4.09
89	207.29	3.41	173.94	3.77
90	221.77	3.18	190.75	3.45
91	236.98	2.94	208.87	3.15
92	253.45	2.70	228.81	2.85
93	272.11	2.44	251.51	2.55
94	295.90	2.17	279.31	2.24
95	329.96	1.87	317.32	1.91
96	384.55	1.54	375.74	1.56
97	480.20	1.20	474.97	1.21
98	657.98	.84	655.85	.84
99	1,000.00	.50	1,000.00	.50
100				
101				
102				
103				
104				
105				
⋮				
115				

TYPES OF INSURANCE POLICIES

Besides life insurance, you can also purchase annuities and endowment contracts from your financial planner or insurance agent. An annuity is a contract with an insurance company: You make regular payments or a lump-sum payment, and the insurance company agrees to pay you income for your lifetime. An annuity pays you while you are alive. Life insurance pays your beneficiaries when you die. Chapter 10 discusses annuities in greater detail.

Endowments are a different breed of life insurance that you don't see much of any more. The reason: Endowment proceeds can be subject to income tax. A later chapter discusses the ramifications.

You buy insurance coverage for 10 or 20 years or to age 65 with an endowment policy. The money that accumulates in the policy can be paid out to the owner at the maturity date. If the insured dies, the amount that has accumulated in the endowment is paid out to the beneficiary.

As you get older, the risks of death are greater. If you choose a whole life policy, a good chunk of the premium goes into your cash value account. Over the years, the growing cash value helps pay the increasing cost of the death benefit through the magic of compound interest. The cash value you've built up helps pay for the cost of the insurance. When the death benefits are paid out, part of the payout represents the cash value, and the other part represents the insurance.

Suppose you have paid your premiums on a $100,000 life insurance policy for 25 years. If you die in the 26th year of the policy, your beneficiaries will collect the $100,000—but $90,000 of it may represent the growth of your cash value and $10,000 its death benefits (see Figure 1–3).

At that point in time when the total amount of the death proceeds represents the accumulated growth of the cash value component of the policy, the policy is said to endow. The policyholder is usually around age 90 or 100 when this happens, so most of us won't have to worry about it—at least according to the mortality charts.

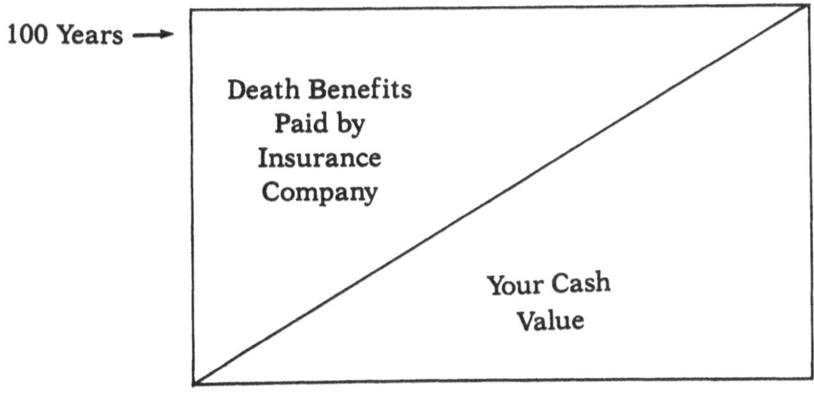

Figure 1–3
Sources of death benefits on whole life insurance.

If you opt to buy a term policy, the insurance company (or you) pay for the risk factor in another way. Younger people pay lower premiums. For example, someone who is age 35 will pay about $560 per year for $400,000 in coverage; a 55-year-old will pay $1,760; and a 65-year-old has to come up with $3,740. The size and age of the risk pool are factors here.

WHO QUALIFIES FOR LIFE INSURANCE?

You have to be in reasonably good health to take out an insurance policy. Generally, insurance companies won't insure people who are in bad health because the risk of a sudden death is too great. Some people in a high-risk occupation (e.g., high-rise construction) or with certain health problems (e.g., a heart murmur or high blood pressure) can get insurance, however.

An insurance company determines whether you are a good risk by reviewing important personal factors through an underwriting process. In life insurance lingo, underwriting means that someone—an underwriter—reviews your application and looks at these health factors:

- Age.
- Build, height, weight, and distribution of weight.
- Physical condition.
- Personal history—health records. Insurance companies also give you a blood test to check for the human immunodeficiency virus (HIV) that causes AIDS. If you are infected, you will not qualify for life insurance coverage.
- The family health history.
- Occupation.
- Habits (e.g., smoking).
- Morals. If your morality affects your lifestyle in a hazardous way or if you misstate the facts when you buy a policy, you may be disqualified.
- Gender. There may be differences in the premiums paid depending on your sex.
- Type of insurance you want.
- Financial condition.
- Involvement in aviation or the military.
- Residence. Where you live has a bearing on your insurability. If you live in a dangerous place overseas, it could affect your rate.
- Hobbies (e.g., race car driving or skydiving).
- Insurance coverage on other family members.

Underwriters are insurance professionals who determine whether it's a good bet to insure you. They look at what is called in the profession the "actuarial cost of providing you with a specific death benefit." In plain English, this means that through years of experience of profiling people, underwriters get a fix on how long you are likely to live based on the law of averages and what you should pay for insurance.

Industry statistics reveal that 93 percent of the people who apply for insurance are accepted at the "standard rate." That means they are expected to live a normal lifetime. About 5 percent are accepted as a higher risk. Only about 2 percent of the applicants don't qualify.

It Pays to Be Healthy

If you like to leap tall buildings in a single bound, a life insurance company may consider you a high-risk candidate—and charge more for your insurance. People that are in exceptionally good health may qualify for preferred rates.

Each insurance company has slightly different underwriting standards. Some firms use a rating system and give you a score. For example, one person might get 10 points subtracted from his or her score because of a good family history, 20 points might be added back because the person is overweight.

Insurable Interest

Another important factor companies look at is called "insurable interest." In essence, this means that an extra careful review will be given to the application of someone who applies for an abnormally large amount of insurance on his or her own life or the life of another person. One person can only insure the life of another if he or she has a financial interest in the continued life of that person. For example, a husband can buy an insurance policy on his wife, but he generally cannot purchase a policy on his neighbor's life.

TYPES OF INSURANCE COMPANIES

Not all life insurance companies are alike. There are two basic types of companies:

1. Mutual life insurance companies, which are owned by the policyholders. These companies sell participating policies. This means that if the insurance company makes profitable investments and keeps (or has) expenses below expectations (lower mortality than projected), it pays dividends to its policyholders.
2. Publicly owned stock companies, which are owned by the shareholders. These companies sell nonparticipating policies.

Nonparticipating Policies

Most nonparticipating policies set fixed premiums on the basis of what the company believes it will cost to provide the insurance coverage. Some newer nonparticipating policies change the amount of the premium periodically, for example, every year, every two years, or every five years. A maximum rate is stated in the policy. Publicly owned insurance companies show a profit to their shareholders when their mortality rates and their expenses are less than expected.

Participating Policies

Participating policies are a little different. Policyholders generally pay higher premiums to allow for fluctuations in company earnings and expenses. At the end of each policy year, though, the company computes its actual costs and refunds any portion of the premium it does not need. The refund, which is called a policy dividend, is not taxable. People who buy participating policies choose what to do with their dividends:

- Invest the dividends in a savings or cash value account.
- Use the dividends for part or all of the premium.
- Use the dividends to buy more insurance (i.e., "paid up insurance"). This tactic helps coverage keep pace with inflation.
- Take the dividends in cash. Although there is no income tax on the dividends, the interest earned on any dividend income is taxable.

The catch is that there's no guarantee that the insurance company will pay dividends. If business is bad and the insurance company's earnings are poor, the company may not pay dividends at all or it may pay lower dividends than the insurance agent projected.

What exactly is the cash value of my policy? Is it a savings account, or is it really insurance?

Life insurance is complex. The cash value in your policy grows as you collect interest income over your lifetime. In other words, you are dealing with statistical probabilities regarding death benefits and the time value of money.

Simply put, older people are likelier to die than younger people. Consequently, insurance companies have to have some extra reserves as the pool of insured people gets older. Insurance companies save cash during people's younger years to provide money to pay all those claims when people get older by requiring them to prepay their insurance through level premium payments over the life of the policy.

This reserve is the reason for the cash value in the policy. The older you get, the more you accumulate money in a savings account that pays interest and the increasing cost of paying for the death benefit. The accumulated money becomes a major part of your death benefits as you get older.

How does the insurance company pay interest on my cash value policy?

Life insurance companies employ a staff of professional money managers who invest all the policyholders' premiums in a diversified portfolio (e.g., common stock, bonds, and real estate). The insurance company then pays the policyholders based on the earnings on their investments.

Most insurance companies are conservative investors. They don't want to take too much risk, but want to pay decent returns. The firm's money managers do this by evaluating the risks of investing in different assets and diversifying their investments on the basis of their assessment. Their outlook for the economy, including interest rates, real estate prices, and corporate earnings are all factors.

Right now, most whole life policies earn around 6 to 8 percent, tax deferred. According to industry statistics, the insurance companies did this by investing their assets—that's all the money they collect from policyholders plus their earnings—as follows:

- Corporate bonds—40 percent.
- U.S. government bonds—17 percent.
- Real estate—3 percent.
- Mortgages—17 percent.
- Policy loans—4 percent.
- Stocks and other investments—19 percent.

DIFFERENT KINDS OF POLICIES SERVE DIFFERENT PURPOSES

Life insurance was once used only to protect the family in the event of the breadwinner's death. The insurance proceeds substituted for the lost income of the wage earner. That's all changed. Insurance companies have come out with more enticing products and the new tax laws make cash buildup on policies one of the few ways to defer paying taxes. In addition, more people are using life insurance to supplement their retirement income. They are tapping their cash value during their senior years.

Later chapters explain how each type of insurance works and what's best for you. For now, here is a rundown of the types of insurance available:

▶ Term Insurance

Term insurance provides limited protection for a specified period of time, although some policies are renewable. Neither health nor occupation affect the renewability feature, but the premium goes up each time the policy is renewed. Some term policies are convertible. Once a policy is converted, cash value begins to build up. In addition, a new physical exam may not be required.

Nothing is paid to beneficiaries of term insurance if the policyholder outlives the policy term unless the policy is converted into a new permanent life policy. If death occurs while the policy is in force, the beneficiaries collect the designated face amount. For a few hundred dollars a year, a younger policyholder can insure his or her family for a hefty sum at a relatively cheap cost. Unlike other types of life insurance, term insurance does not generate cash value.

- *Level Term* provides a fixed amount of insurance for a specified period of time, for example, $100,000 of death benefits for 10 years. You can also set up a term policy so that the premiums increase in stages. That way the insurance is more affordable during the early policy years.
- *Decreasing term* drops in value from year to year. You get less coverage as time goes by, but the premiums stay level during the life of the policy. This type of insurance often is used to cover the declining amount on a home mortgage.
- *Increasing term* means that the death benefits increase over specific time periods.

▶ Whole Life Insurance

People buy whole life insurance if they want permanent life insurance. Monthly payments or premiums are made to fund a specific death benefit, and the payments earn interest or cash value over the years. The most common type of whole life is called straight life. The same premium is paid every year. The premiums generally are higher than regular term insurance and lower than renewable term.

Some policies let you pay premiums over a 20-year period (or less). The earnings on the cash value and the dividends you earn over that time are used to pay part of your premiums. The result is that your policy is paid up early. However, this assumes that the insurance company's estimates are realized. This type of insurance is called "vanishing premium whole life insurance."

Another feature of this type of policy is that its cash value can be used to obtain a low-cost loan. Today, it could cost you 8 percent or more to borrow from your policy. However, you are actually paying less for the loan because your cash value will earn 2 percent less than the loan rate the insurance company charges you. For example, assume the following: You borrow $10,000 from your life insurance policy at 8 percent interest. Your cash value, however, now earns 6 percent; so in reality, you only pay 2 percent net interest on the loan. This is called "2 percent net interest."

▶ Universal Life Insurance

Universal life was created when interest rates skyrocketed during the 1980s. It is essentially a whole life, or permanent, policy that allows flexible premium payments. Policyholders who have pressing financial needs or limited income and cash flow can vary the amount and timing of their premium payments.

The insurance company invests the funds it collects in the short-term money and bond markets within the cash value component of the policy. A certain death benefit is guaranteed. Under one form of universal life, if the cash value grows at high rates, the death benefits even increase.

▶ Excess Interest Whole Life Insurance

In this variation on a universal life policy, the premium payments and death benefits are fixed. The cash value fluctuates with market conditions. Consequently, if market conditions are favorable and the premiums paid in the first few years of the policy are large enough, you may not have to pay any premiums after a certain point in time.

▶ Variable Life Insurance

Variable life insurance offers yet a different twist. Like whole life, it offers permanent insurance coverages. However, the policyholder—not the insurance company—assumes the investment risk. The choice of investment includes money market accounts, bond funds, and various types of stock mutual funds. Since the amount of the cash buildup changes with the performance of the investment, the earnings and death benefits of the policy above the floor amount guaranteed by the insurance company will vary.

▶ Single Premium Life Insurance

Single premium life insurance requires only one premium payment. The insurance company pays death benefits, and your money earns a fixed rate based on the prevailing market. In a single premium variable life insurance policy, you have a choice of investing in a mutual fund in hopes of raising the cash value of the policy. The amount of the death benefit is determined partly by the investment results of the mutual funds.

▶ Adjustable Life Insurance

This type of policy lets you change your mind. If your goals and financial conditions change, you can adjust your insurance policy. If you want to increase or decrease your coverage, you can either change your premium payments or change the length of time the policy is in force. You may have to show evidence of insurability if you are increasing the death benefits.

The following list summarizes the characteristics of the various types of life insurance:[1]

[1] Information for this list was obtained from the American Council of Life Insurance.

Term

- Protection for a specified time.
- Renewal and convertible into whole life insurance.
- Low initial premium.
- Increased premium for each new term.
- No cash value.

Whole Life

- Permanent protection.
- Fixed premium.
- Fixed death benefit.
- Fixed cash value.
- Tax-free policy earnings while the policy is in force.

Universal Life

- Permanent protection.
- Flexible premium.
- Flexible death benefits.
- Cash value based on the premiums paid and market conditions.
- Tax-free policy earnings while the policy is in force.

Excess Interest Whole Life

- Permanent protection.
- Fixed premium, but can be adjusted by the insurance company after issue.
- Fixed death benefits.
- Cash value growth dependent on market conditions.
- Temporary elimination of premiums if investment results are favorable.
- Tax-free policy earnings while the policy is in force.

Variable Life

- Permanent protection.
- Fixed or flexible premiums.

- Policyholders control the investment of their separate stock, bond, money market, and other mutual fund accounts.
- Death benefits and cash value vary in relation to the performance of the mutual funds in the separate accounts.

Adjustable Life

- Permanent protection.
- Death benefit that can be raised or lowered.
- Premium that can be increased or decreased.
- Protection period that can be lengthened or shortened.
- Earnings generated by the policy are not taxed while the policy is in force.

SPECIAL POLICIES

A nice thing about life insurance is that policies are adaptable enough to accommodate most lifestyles, financial conditions, and needs. Some of the most common variations, which we will discuss in more detail in later chapters, include the following:

- *Whole Life with Family Riders.* A combination of whole life and decreasing-term insurance policies, this arrangement provides monthly income to a young family for a lifetime. If the policyholder dies, the survivor gets a lump-sum death benefit from the whole life policy. The decreasing-term insurance then pays monthly income for a specified time (e.g., 20 years).
- *Modified Life.* A whole life policy for people who don't have a lot of money now but expect their income to grow over the years. A young couple, for example, would pay low premiums for the first few years of the policy. Later on, however, they would pay higher than normal whole life premiums for their insurance coverage.
- *Family Policies.* An all-in-one plan that allows everyone to get into the act. Under one contract, the husband, wife, and

dependent children get insurance protection in one package. The children might get term insurance that's convertible to whole life at age 21. One spouse may have whole life and the other term.

SPECIAL POLICY RIDERS AND CLAUSES

Life insurance companies try to lessen their risk and protect themselves by including certain clauses in their policies. One example is a suicide clause. Life insurance contracts can also be tailored to meet particular conditions such as an accidental death or injury. These modifications or changes are known as "riders."

Some of the more common riders and policy clauses are:

- *Incontestability Clause.* After you have had the policy for two years, the insurance company cannot cancel your policy because it learns some of the information you provided was wrong. For example, suppose you told the insurance company you were a nonsmoker even though you really smoke three packs a day. If the insurance company finds out that you lied after one year, your policy can be canceled. If you pass as a nonsmoker for two years, your coverage cannot be terminated.
- *Double Indemnity or Accidental Death Benefits.* If the policyholder dies in an accident, the survivors collect double the death benefit.
- *Suicide Clauses.* If the policyholder commits suicide during the first two years of the policy, the beneficiaries only collect the total amount of the premiums paid into the policy. After two years, suicide is covered by the insurance company.
- *Automatic Premium Loan Provision.* The insurance company pays outstanding premiums as a loan against the cash value in your policy.

- *Waiver of Premium.* If you get injured on the job or disabled in any way, your payments are waived for the entire time you are disabled.
- *Disability Income.* This rider pays a specific amount of supplemental income if you become disabled for a specific period.
- *Guaranteed Insurability.* You can buy more insurance in the future without a medical exam. Insurance can be purchased up to the contract age limit (usually age 40) without proof of insurability.
- *Family Riders.* Family term insurance can be bought along with your whole life coverage. You can also get temporary term coverage for the entire clan.
- *Misstatement of Age Provision.* If the insurance company finds out that you are older than you told them you were, the company will pay benefits based on the premium payments made and the amount of death benefit you would have been covered by based on your real age.

Nonforfeiture Options

What happens if you can't make any more payments and your policy doesn't have a waiver of premium or disability income rider? You have to talk to your agent about termination of your policy or nonforfeiture options. Some of the possible choices are:

- Terminate the policy and use the cash value to buy either extended term insurance or paid up insurance. In both cases, the amount of insurance you can get is determined by the cash value you put down as a single premium, your age when the original policy was taken out, and the rates charged for a person your current age. Additional proof of insurability is not required.

Borrowing against the Cash Value

Policyholders can borrow against the cash value of their life insurance policies at lower rates (usually about 8 percent).

Insurance companies are required to loan you the cash value you have accumulated in your policy without a credit check. They have collateral—your cash. The loan does not have to be paid back, but it's a good idea to pay it back anyway because the death benefits are decreased by the amount of the loan plus accrued interest. For example, suppose the face amount of your policy is $100,000. You borrow the $50,000 cash value of the policy to pay for your twin daughters' college education. If you suddenly die before repaying that amount, your beneficiaries will only get $50,000.

- *The 10-Day Free Trial.* You can change your mind after you buy a policy. You have 10 days after you sign on the bottom line and pay your premium to look over the policy and decide whether you really want it.
- *The Grace Period.* Policyholders get 31 days after each premium's due date to make their payments. Your coverage is in force during this hiatus. However, if the policyholder dies during the grace period, the premium due is deducted from the death benefits.

Settlement Options

Most people have to save a lifetime to create a fund for their heirs. For example, someone who puts $4,000 a year into a whole life policy that pays 8 percent tax deferred, will have over $350,000 in 20 years. Alternatively, a similar vehicle can be used to provide $30,000 in annuity income beginning at age 65.

There are many different types of settlement options for the payment of benefits. Detailed descriptions of all these options are explained in later chapters. The following paragraphs offer a brief summary:

- *Interest Option.* The death benefit money is left with the insurance company, and the interest earned on that amount is paid out to the beneficiary. The beneficiary can take out part or all of the proceeds in cash, if that's part of the contract set up by the policyowner.

- *Regular Payouts..* The proceeds are paid out in installments over time. This is also known as the *life only* option. Chapter 13 discusses this option in greater detail.
- *Life Income Option.* The death benefits can be received by taking the income for as long as the beneficiary lives or for a certain period of time such as 5, 10, 15, or 20 years.

Can insurance be used to save money for the future?

Yes. Many financially unsophisticated consumers buy whole life insurance policies for just this purpose. A policy that pays 6 percent interest—not taxable, remember—will grow at a taxable equivalent rate of 8.3 percent for taxpayers in the 28 percent tax bracket.

Why not buy term insurance and invest the difference in mutual funds?

Critics point out that other investments pay more. For example, according to the Wiesenberger Investment Company Service, someone who invested $10,000 in the Investment Company of America Fund in 1940 would have accumulated $3,899,383 by 1990. The annual rate of growth was 12.67 percent. That sounds great. But how many people had $10,000 to invest in 1940? The same is true today. Most of us don't have a lump sum available for investment purposes. Buying life insurance can serve the same function. Even though you earn less money, you will have to make payments so your policy remains in effect. This can be viewed as an enforced savings program. For many, the trade-off is worth it.

POINTS TO REMEMBER

- You buy life insurance for income protection.
- Term insurance is only low-cost protection when you are young. It gets more expensive as you get older.
- Whole life insurance is permanent protection. Part of your premium is used to buy insurance, part goes into an interest-bearing savings account.
- Participating insurance is issued by mutual insurance companies. Mutual insurance companies are owned by their policyholders. Policyholders typically receive annual dividends.
- If you buy a universal life insurance policy, you can determine how much must be paid in premiums every year.
- With a variable life insurance policy, your cash value can be invested in common stock and bond mutual funds.
- After you buy the policy, you have 10 days to look it over. If you don't like the policy, the insurance company will refund your money.
- You can borrow against the cash value in your insurance policy at low rates and without a credit check.
- You don't pay state or federal income tax on the cash value buildup in your insurance policy.

2

How Much Life Insurance Do You Need?

TAKE YOUR FINANCIAL TEMPERATURE

Insurance should be part of a well-designed financial plan. It is worth taking the time to assess your net worth, review your spending habits, determine how much you need to save for your retirement, and figure out how you will pay for your children's education before deciding how much life insurance you need or calling in an insurance agent. Most financial planners say you should buy life insurance at an early age during your working years. You need to save about 5 to 15 percent of your gross income to meet your financial needs over the long term. Part of your savings plan should include buying life insurance that is equivalent to about 5 to 8 times your current wages. So if you make $50,000 a year, you should have between $250,000 and $400,000 of coverage, as a general rule of thumb.

Zeroing In on Your Financial Needs and Goals

The United States Treasury can print all the money it needs. Average citizens can't. The only way they can build wealth is by taking a hard look at their financial goals—and then start saving toward them.

The first step in this process is taking a financial inventory.

Sit down and make a list of your short-term, intermediate, and long-term goals, along with the date and estimated cost of meeting those objectives. Short-term goals might include saving three to six months' income as an emergency fund or for a down payment on a car. Intermediate goals include items such as a down payment for a house. Long-term goals include saving for retirement.

Next, create a balance sheet listing your assets and liabilities. Assets are what you own—liabilities are what you owe.

Cutting the Fat out of the Family Budget

After you have a fix on what you're worth, look at how much you spend.

Write down, item by item, all the money you spent this week. You'll be surprised at how much it adds up to—that extra cup of coffee at the diner around the corner, magazines, and so on. Then leaf through your checkbook and make an itemized list of your income and expenses for the year. Divide that amount by 12 to give you a monthly figure. Next, figure out where you can cut.

Wealth Building Worksheet

Use this balance sheet to figure your net worth.

Assets		
Financial assets		
Cash and checking accounts		
Savings accounts		
Certificates of deposit		
Stocks and bonds		
Life insurance cash value		
Mutual funds		
Collectibles		
Real estate		
Loans owed to you		
Other		
Total financial assets		
Nonliquid assets		
Home		
Auto		
Household furnishings		
Equity in business		
Other		
Total fixed assets		
Future assets		
Company pension		
IRA		
Keogh		
Other		
Total future assets		
Grand total assets		
Liabilities		
Home mortgage		
Other real estate		
Installment credit		
Auto		
Furniture		
Home improvement		
Education		
Clothing		
Other debts		
Total liabilities		
Net worth (assets less liabilities)		

Wealth Building Worksheet

Use this worksheet to see if you are spending more than you are earning. This will also give you a good idea about how much life insurance you can afford.

Income		
Take-home pay	______	
Other income	______	
Total monthly income		______
Fixed monthly expenses		
Savings and investing	______	
House or rent	______	
Car and transportation	______	
Other debt payments	______	
Food	______	
Utilities	______	
Child care	______	
Other	______	
Subtotal	______	
Variable monthly expenses		
Federal and state tax payments	______	
All types of insurance payments	______	
House repairs	______	
Car repairs	______	
Medical	______	
Other	______	
Subtotal	______	
Total monthly expenses		______
Extra (income less expenses)		======

RECLAIM WASTEFUL SPENDING

After you've completed the balance sheet and budget worksheet, examine them carefully. You may find that your debts are growing faster than your assets. If you're often in the red, ask yourself why. Was there a financial emergency, such as a leaky roof? Or did you make unnecessary purchases—perhaps a shiny new European sports car? Either way, your analysis should give you a good idea where you can cut nonessential spending. These data provide widely used standard rules of thumb.

Look at the following annual percentages of how much, after taxes, you should be spending on line items in your budget. (These percentages should be adjusted to meet local conditions. For example, housing costs more in New York City than in Des Moines, Iowa.)

- Housing, including interest, principal, and taxes: to 25 percent
- Food: 13 percent
- Life Insurance: 6 percent
- Transportation: 6 percent
- Credit cards and installment debt: 20 percent or less
- Entertainment and travel: 5 percent
- Clothing: 6 percent
- Savings: 5 to 20 percent
- Medical expenses: Vary with age and health

You should also review your most recent tax return. Multiply your after-tax income by each of the preceding percentages. Divide that amount by 12 to arrive at a hypothetical monthly budget. Compare your monthly expenses with your monthly budget. If your expenses are more than your budget, you can see where you are overspending.

You probably found that you can save a lot of money by cutting impulse purchases at the grocery store and the department store, trimming entertainment expenses, and using the public library instead of buying paperbacks. It may even be possible to save by using public transportation to commute to work. If you're paying too much in credit card interest, pay off the debt—a painful but financially laudable move. One alternative in this area is looking for a charge card that charges a lower rate and transferring your debt to that card. Another option is to consolidate your debts by getting a secured loan at the bank—perhaps even a home equity loan.

Taking these steps might yield as much as an extra $200 a month to invest. If your financial position is too serious to control yourself, consider hiring a financial planner. Both the Institute of Certified Financial Planners, 7600 Eastman Avenue, Suite 301, Denver, CO 80231, and the International Association for Financial Planning, 2 Concourse Parkway, Atlanta, GA 30328, will send you a list of planners in your area.

THE TIME VALUE OF MONEY

Once you've made up your mind to set your financial game plan into action, you can sit back and assess how much your savings will grow. For example, suppose you expect to need $40,000 in 10 years to pay for Junior's college education. Check Table 2–1 to figure out how much you have to save each month to achieve your goal.

HOW MUCH INSURANCE DO YOU NEED?

How much insurance do you need? You need enough to maintain your family's current standard of living for several years. There are several ways to zero in on the "right" amount. One

Table 2–1
Earnings Based on $100 per Month over 30 Years at Various Interest Rates

	Annual Rate of Return				
Number of Years	*5%*	*8%*	*10%*	*12%*	*15%*
5	$ 6,829	$ 7,397	$ 7,808	$ 8,247	$ 8,968
10	15,592	18,417	20,655	23,334	27,866
15	26,840	34,835	41,792	50,458	67,686
20	41,275	59,295	76,570	99,915	151,595
25	59,799	95,737	133,789	189,764	328,407
30	83,573	150,030	277,933	352,991	700,982

popular rule of thumb is that you need about five to eight times your annual income to protect your family. You can make another, more precise assessment by using the multiples of salary approach developed by Citibank about 15 years ago. A still more detailed approach, called a capital needs analysis, looks at your net worth or assets less liabilities, your current income and expenses, your forecasted income and expenses, and what the family will have after your death including burial expenses, Social Security, and other sources of income.

The "Salary × Five" Approach

While you are waiting for the morning commuter train or bus, you can get a quick fix on how much insurance you need. Just multiply your current annual wages by five. This rule of thumb gives you an idea how much coverage you need. It assumes that five times your wages will be adequate coverage even with inflation. Surprisingly, some experts note that after the insurance agent collects all your data and does an analysis, the computer comes up with about five to eight times your wages.

Table 2–2 will give you some idea of how much you need based on multiplying your income by five or eight.

Table 2–2
Salary × Five Approach

	Amount of Insurance	
Income	*5×*	*8×*
$ 25,000	$125,000	$200,000
35,000	175,000	280,000
45,000	225,000	360,000
55,000	275,000	440,000
65,000	325,000	520,000
75,000	375,000	600,000
95,000	475,000	760,000
105,000	525,000	840,000

Multiples-of-Salary Method

The multiples-of-salary approach takes into account other sources of income in figuring insurance coverage. This method assumes the family lives on about 75 percent of the after-tax income of the breadwinner. These estimates assume a family of 4, and the proceeds would be invested at 5 percent interest after taxes and inflation. This method assumes the family gets Social Security.

Let's say your spouse is 45 years old and your gross income is $65,000: Table 2–3 shows you that to have 75 percent of your present income, you multiply 7.5 times your wages. So you need about $488,000 in face-value life insurance to provide your survivors with 75 percent of your after-tax income. The factor is 5.5 at 60 percent of your current after-tax income. That translates into $357,500 of coverage.

An Expert's View

Jonathan Pond, Certified Financial Planner (CFP), a highly respected financial planner and president of Financial Planning Information, Inc., Watertown, MA, tells his clients, "The

Table 2–3
Citibank's Multiples-of-Salary

Your Present Gross Earnings	*Present Age of Spouse*							
	25 Years		*35 Years*		*45 Years*		*55 Years*	
	75%	*60%*	*75%*	*60%*	*75%*	*60%*	*75%*	*60%*
$ 7,500	4.0	3.0	5.5	4.0	7.5	5.5	6.5	4.5
9,000	4.0	3.0	5.6	4.0	7.5	5.5	6.5	4.5
15,000	4.5	3.0	6.5	4.5	8.0	6.0	7.0	5.5
23,500	6.5	4.5	8.0	5.5	8.6	6.5	7.5	5.5
30,000	7.5	5.0	8.0	6.0	8.5	6.5	7.0	5.5
40,000	7.5	5.0	8.0	6.0	8.0	6.0	7.0	5.5
65,000	7.5	5.5	7.5	6.0	7.5	6.0	6.5	5.0

Source: "Consumer Views," Citibank, July 1976. By courtesy of "Consumer Views," published by Citibank, copyright Citicorp.

Wealth Building Worksheet

Life Insurance Needs

Note: All amounts should be expressed in current dollars.

Expenses

1. Final expenses (one-time expenses incurred by your death)
   a. Final illness (medical costs will probably exceed health insurance deductibles and coinsurance, so assume you will have to fund at least those amounts) $________
   b. Burial/funeral costs ________
   c. Probate costs (if unsure, assume 4% of assets passing through probate process) ________
   d. Federal estate taxes (for most estates, over $600,000 willed to someone other than spouse) ________
   e. State inheritance taxes (varies by state) ________
   f. Legal fees, estate administration ________
   g. Other ________
   h. Total final expenses ________
2. Outstanding debt (to be paid off at your death)
   a. Credit card/consumer debt ________
   b. Car ________
   c. Mortgage (if it's to be paid off at your death, otherwise include payments in life income) ________
   d. Other ________
   e. Total outstanding debt ________

Wealth Building Worksheet *(cont'd)*

3. Readjustment expenses (to cover the transition period of immediate crisis)
   a. Child care ________
   b. Additional homemaking help ________
   c. Vocational counseling/educational training (for a nonworking or underemployed spouse who expects to seek paid employment) ________
   d. Other ________
   e. Total readjustment expenses ________
4. Dependency expenses (until all children are self-supporting)
   a. Estimate your household's current annual expenditures ________
   b. To remove the deceased's expenses, multiply this figure by:
      .70 for a surviving family of one
      .74 for a surviving family of two
      .78 for a surviving family of three
      .80 for a surviving family of four
      .82 for a surviving family of five
      $_____ (Line 4a) – *x* (factor) = ________
   c. Deduct spouse's estimated annual income from employment (________)
   d. Equals current annual expenses to be covered by currently owned assets and insurance ________

Wealth Building Worksheet *(cont'd)*

e. To determine approximate total dependency expenses required, multiply by number of years until youngest child becomes self-supporting: $_____ (Line 4bf) × _____ (years) = ________

f. If support for dependent parent(s) is to be provided, multiply annual support by the number of years such support is expected to continue: $_____ × _____ (years) = ________

g. Total dependency expenses (add Lines 4e and 4f) ________

5. Education expenses

a. Annual private school tuition in current dollars (if desired) ________

b. Multiply by number of years children have left to attend: $_____ (Line 5a) × _____ (years) = ________

c. Annual college costs in current dollars ________

d. Multiply by number of years and children left to attend: $_____ (Line 5c) × _____ (years) = ________

e. Total education expenses (add Lines 5b + 5d) ________

6. Life income (for the surviving spouse after the children are all self-supporting)

a. Annual amount desired (in current dollars) ________

Wealth Building Worksheet *(cont'd)*

b. Deduct spouse's estimated annual income from employment (________)

c. Equals annual expenses to be covered by currently owned assets and insurance ________

d. Multiply by number of years between when the youngest child becomes self-supporting and the surviving spouse begins receiving Social Security benefits and other retirement income, if any: $______ (Line 6c) × ______ (years) = ________

7. Retirement income for surviving spouse

a. Annual amount desired in current dollars less Social Security and any pension income ________

b. Multiply by number of years of life expectancy after retirement begins: $______ (Line 7a) × ______ (years) = ________

8. Total funds needed to cover expenses: (add lines 1h, 2e, 3e, 4g, 5e, 6d, 7b) ________

Assets Currently Available to Support Family

Proceeds from life insurance already owned ________

Cash and savings ________

Equity in real estate (if survivors will sell) ________

Securities ________

Wealth Building Worksheet *(cont'd)*

IRA and Keogh plans	________	
Employer savings plans	________	
Lump-sum employer pension benefits	________	
Other sources	________	
9. Total assets		________

Additional Life Insurance Required

10. Subtract available-assets (Line 9) from total funds needed to cover expenses (Line 8). If Line 10 is positive, it represents the approximate additional insurance needed	________

best way to determine how much insurance is enough is to estimate how much money you would need to take care of all your dependents' financial needs.

"Once you know that," he adds, "you can judge whether a lesser amount might be more appropriate." Pond put together the following Wealth Building Worksheet.

It's worth the time and energy to review your financial condition and insurance needs. That way, you can be sure that you are only buying what you need.

WEALTH BUILDING PROFILE ***Couple Sets Up Budget.*** The Mulligans have an after-tax income of $68,400. They are in their mid-30's and have one child, age 7. The couple are faithful savers, but have racked up a large credit card balance. The couple met with a financial planner who helped them get their finances under control. They paid off their charges from their savings and set up a budget. Based on their streamlined budget, the Mulligans spend $14,000 a year for their home mortgage, $8,892 for food, $4,000 for transportation, $4,000 for entertainment and vacations, and $5,000 for clothes. They also save $3,000 a year outside their company pension plans. As a result, the Mulligans had enough extra money to buy a $250,000 life insurance policy.

POINTS TO REMEMBER

- Write down a list of your financial needs and goals.
- Figure out how much you can afford to pay for life insurance by looking at your income and expenses for the past few years.
- Set up a budget and cut wasteful spending.
- Meet with a financial planner to help you set up an appropriate financial plan that will meet your goals, whether they are funding a comfortable retirement or paying for a child's education expenses.
- Most people need between five and eight times their current wages to have adequate life insurance protection.

3

Find an Insurance Agent—And a Sound Insurance Company

LET THE BUYER BEWARE

Consumer Reports conducted an investigative study in 1986 that revealed several rather alarming facts:[1]

- A number of unscrupulous agents tried to sell high-commission products instead of what the reporter needed.
- Some of the agents tried to discourage the reporter from shopping around for the best policy at the best price. "Trust me," they said.
- Most agents promoted the policies the home office was pushing. That meant selling either a cash value whole life or universal life policy. Of the nine agents the reporter talked to, three tried to sell whole life, four pushed universal life, one recommended term insurance, and the other pushed a combination cash value and term policy.
- The dividends some of the agents promised were exaggerated. One agent told the reporter that the dividends from the firm's term policy would accumulate to an astounding

[1] Lieberman, Trudy. *Life Insurance: How to Buy the Right Policy at the Right Price.* Fairfield, OH: Consumer Reports Books, 1988.

$88,000 over 30 years. But dividends from top-rated insurance companies' $100,000 term policies were really $6,500 to $15,000. One agent used an 11 percent interest rate to show how the cash value would grow over the long haul in a universal policy, when in fact interest rates were 10 percent and headed lower.

You can't buy on blind faith. Don't leave important financial decisions up to a stranger, even the one who represents a reputable company. Remember, agents get 50 percent or more in first-year commissions when they sell cash value insurance. After the second year the policy is in force, they get about 2 percent of every premium.

Buy What You Need

Being prepared for the agent's visit will help you determine whether your best interests are important to the agent, or whether the commission is the hook. Do your homework. Read about the kinds of insurance policies financial planners and agents sell. Ask the professional how he or she is compensated.

What's Their Background?

There are other important characteristics to look for in an insurance agent or financial planner. In the old days, you did business with Bud, the local agent who worked for XYZ Neighborhood Insurance Agency on Main Street. Today, we have financial planners—20,000 of them throughout the United States. They are like financial quarterbacks, because they focus on your entire financial ball game.

WHAT YOU CAN EXPECT A FINANCIAL PLANNER OR INSURANCE AGENT TO DO FOR YOU

A good financial planner will help you evaluate your financial needs and make recommendations to improve your financial well-being. A financial planner should assist you with the following:

- Review your finances by looking at past tax returns, investments, retirement savings plans, wills, and life and disability insurance policies.
- Help you discover your savings and investment philosophy.
- Set up a financial game plan to meet your needs and goals.
- Spot financial trouble spots. You may need to pay off debts, put more into retirement, strengthen your investment returns, or obtain more life and disability insurance coverage.
- Develop a detailed and understandable plan to improve your financial security.
- Make recommendations about other financial professionals you may need such as lawyers, accountants, or money managers.
- Provide you with a contract or letter of agreement that describes the services, fees, and terms of the agreement.

CHECK THEIR CREDENTIALS

Anyone can hang out a shingle and claim to be a financial planner. There are no federal or state regulating agencies, so before you hire a planner to help you with your savings and insurance needs, check the person's educational background, work experience, and professional credentials. Important professional designations include the following:

- *Certified Financial Planner (CFP).* The CFP designation is awarded by the International Board of Standards and Practices for Certified Financial Planners (IBCFP), Denver, CO, to candidates who have completed six intensive financial planning courses and passed a national examination. Course work includes training in employee benefits, insurance investments, and tax and estate planning. To keep the CFP license, the financial planner must adhere to a code of ethics as well as meet continuing education requirements.

- *Chartered Life Underwriter (CLU).* Any insurance agent worth his or her salt has a CLU or is working toward getting this designation. And if you find a person with both the CLU and Chartered Financial Consultant (ChFC), you know this person has a strong background in insurance and all aspects of financial planning. Both designations are issued by the American College, Bryn Mawr, PA, to individuals who have passed a national examination based on at least a dozen financial planning related courses. The CLU is required to take courses with a specialty in life insurance and personal insurance planning. The ChFC involves a 10-course program in financial, estate, and tax planning, in addition to investment management.
- *Chartered Property Casualty Underwriter (CPCU).* This agent is required to pass a national examination administered by the Insurance Institute of America, Malvern, PA. To obtain a CPCU, a person must complete a 10-semester curriculum covering a broad range of topics including insurance, risk management, and general business topics.
- *Certified Public Accountant (CPA).* CPAs must pass a national examination, but they are licensed by the state where they set up practice. A CPA candidate must have a bachelor's degree and must have worked for an accounting firm for at least two years.
- *Accredited Personal Financial Planning Specialist (APFS).* This designation is given to CPAs who pass a stringent financial planning examination administered by the American Institute of Certified Public Accountants.
- *Chartered Financial Analyst (CFA).* You probably won't run into a CFA because these professionals primarily work for brokerage firms and analyze companies. To take the CFA exam, candidates must have a college degree and work experience. A passing grade indicates the person has competence in quantitative methods, securities analysis, accounting, and securities law.

- *Fellow, Life Management Institute (FLMI).* This designation is awarded to insurance people by the Life Management Institute of the Life Office Management Association, Atlanta, GA. Someone who has an FLMI must pass six examinations administered by this organization, one of which is a test on strategic management.

GET REFERRALS

You should get referrals for a financial advisor from other professionals, such as lawyers and accountants. Be sure to ask them whether they are receiving a finder's fee for the referral. Be cautious if they are.

Another warning: If you are hiring someone who manages money in addition to peddling insurance, ask your state's Division of Securities whether any complaints have been filed against the person. If the person is a registered investment advisor, ask to see the ADV form. Registered investment advisors must file this form with the Securities & Exchange Commission. The ADV contains important financial information about the advisor, as well as this person's qualifications.

MORE WAYS TO TELL THE GOOD FROM THE BAD

Here's a rundown of other things you should look for in a good agent.

- Does the person listen to you? How does the agent respond to your questions and explain things to you? Does the person restate what you have said back to you? Do you get the feeling the agent understands what you say? Here's a way to spot a good listener:

  The agent may make such remarks as, "I understand this is confusing." Or, "Yes, I understand that this seems like too much coverage. But you also said you want some cash value for a future loan."

Responsiveness is the key. Does the person return your calls right away? Does he or she send you the extra information you request?

Say you want a report on the quarterly performance of the insurance company's stock funds that are in the variable life insurance product: Will your agent get you that information so you can compare the performance of the funds against other mutual funds?

- Does the agent answer your questions or skip over what you say and go on with the sales pitch?
- Does the agent look at your financial history before making recommendations or evaluating your goals and objectives?
- Does the agent explain the fees, charges, and commissions?
- Does the agent show you realistic illustrations or examples?

ACTION ITEM

Write the Institute for Certified Financial Planners, 7600 East Eastman Avenue, Suite 301, Denver, CO 80231. Ask them to send you their booklet, "Selecting a Qualified Financial Planning Professional: Twelve Questions to Consider." Or you can call the Institute for Certified Financial Planners at 800-282-7526 for names of qualified financial planners in your area. Other sources for free information on how to pick a financial planner include the American Association of Retired Persons Consumer Affairs Section, 1909 K Street, NW, Washington, DC 20049. The International Association for Financial Planning (IAFP), 2 Concourse Parkway, Atlanta, GA 30328, has a consumer referral program. You can get a list of planners in your area by calling 800-945-IAFP.

SELECTING A "SOLID GOLD" INSURANCE COMPANY

Don't settle for anything less than the financially strongest insurance companies that offer the best prices with the best records of paying dividends or distribution earnings. When making your selection, keep in mind that past performance is not always an indication of future results. To go with a safe company, it might be worth paying slightly higher fees or earning a little bit lower rates on your cash value. Remember, insurance products are not insured by Uncle Sam against default, so safety is important—especially in today's uncertain economic environment.

If you put money in a high-yielding bank or thrift CD and the institution goes out of business, you are protected up to $100,000 per person by the Federal Deposit Insurance Corporation (FDIC). But when you buy life insurance, you get no federal government guarantees. You must rely on the management of the insurance company to earn money at a low risk, so they can pay claims and interest on your cash value.

As discussed later in this chapter, each state has a guarantee association with an insurance fund to protect policyholders in the event their insurance company goes out of business. Nevertheless, it is not the same as a bank deposit insured through the FDIC. The money is used to cover death benefits and cash values in the event an insurance company defaults.

HIGH YIELDS MEAN BIG RISKS

Many consumers and experts are concerned about the safety of the insurance industry because of the slumping real estate and junk bond markets. In the early 1980s, consumers lost money when they bought annuities issued by Baldwin United Corporation, which held $3.9 billion in assets. Thousands of policyholders were saved when Metropolitan Life Insurance Company bought much of Baldwin's business. Consumers put money into a Baldwin United annuity that promised to pay excessively high, tax-free returns until the purchaser's retirement. In the end, people had to settle for much less. So much for that pie-in-the-sky source of lifetime income you are supposed to get from an insurance company.

Look at what has happened so far in the 1990s. Two of the largest insurance companies in the country—Equitable Life and Executive Life—are in financial hot water. Equitable's problems developed because it tried to stay competitive by offering high returns on its products. In the early 1980s, the company paid a lot more than its competitors on cash value insurance. When the high-yield bond market dropped and interest rates dropped, corporate profits were squeezed. The firm's real estate portfolio soured, too. Now Equitable is restructuring and is hopeful that $1 billion in cash from AXA, a French Insurance Group will allow it to continue functioning.

Executive Life also was trapped by the big losses in the junk bond market. (Junk bonds are issued by companies that pay high returns to compensate investors for the risk of investing in a weak company.) Over 70 percent of Executive Life's portfolio was invested in junk bonds. Guess what happened. The market value of Executive's $13 billion in assets plunged. The firm's investment portfolio lost $900 million in 1990. When policyholders learned about the problem, many cashed out. The firm paid out almost $4 billion in policy redemptions from frightened policyholders.

State regulators stepped in and stopped the firm from selling new policies, and the company was ordered to beef up its cash reserves. When the company went under, California's Department of Insurance took control. The insurance regulator put Executive Life under court supervision and began a search for a buyer. In early 1992, a French insurance company that goes by the acronym MAAS received final court approval to acquire the bankrupt insurance company. Policies over $100,000 may not get 100 cents on the dollar. At the time of this writing, the court was deciding how much policyholders will get.

Despite these problems, the American Council of Life Insurance, a trade group based in Washington, DC, says the state guarantee associations are protecting Executive Life's policyholders. Ninety-five percent of the policyholders will have received 100 percent of their death benefits and cash values. Only a few speculators may not get all or part of their money returned. The *Wall Street Journal* reported that some of Executive's policyholders have coverage above the guarantee association limits. In addition, pension funds that invested in the firm's guaranteed investment contracts may not be protected against losses.

HOW HEALTHY IS THE INDUSTRY?

A report in 1991 by IDS Life Insurance Company, Minneapolis, MN, said that "one fifth of the largest U.S. insurance companies risk insolvency in a severe economic downturn or market decline." A 1991 report by Standard & Poor's (S&P) confirms that the industry is coming under pressure. S&P believes that a number of insurance companies "have stretched their capital to levels that have affected credit quality." In other words, the firm's money in their coffers to cover losses is getting slimmer than S&P thinks is advisable. In plain English, this means there is no free lunch when you buy insurance. That's not to say that every major insurance company is going to go bankrupt.

Analyst Larry Brossman, vice president of Duff & Phelps Credit Rating Company, Chicago, IL, emphasizes that the industry, as a group, is financially sound. Still, about 6 percent of the mortgages in insurance portfolios have problems. Brossman believes that only about half of the 2,000 insurance companies in business today will be business 15 years from now.

Today's Insurance Companies Are Stronger

We've been through a rough couple of years. But now policyholders can breathe a sigh of relief. Life insurance companies are rebuilding their financial strength after the recession.

According to a study published by Weiss Research, West Palm Beach, FL, the life and health insurance industry is recovering its financial footing, despite continued difficulties with troubled real estate and mortgages. The study, based on September 1992 data, shows that most insurance companies' assets and capital are growing. In addition, fewer policyholders are cashing out their life insurance.

Another study by the American Council of Life Insurance (ACLI), Washington, DC, also reveals insurance companies are slowly getting out from under their bad real estate problems. Delinquent loans accounted for 6.37 percent of insurers' mortgage portfolios by year-end 1992 or just 1.1 percent of assets. That figure is down from 7.12 percent and 7.27 percent in the second and third quarters of last year, respectively.

In addition, ACLI statistics show: Mortgage holdings fell to an all-time low of 15.2 percent of assets at year-end 1992, down from 19.2 percent in 1990; Insurance companies have increased their investments in mortgage-backed securities and cut back new investments in junk bonds. New commitments on privately placed bonds rated BB or below are 3.9 percent, compared with 6.2 percent of insurance companies' investments in 1991.

A greater percentage of insurance companies' investments are going into U.S. government securities and investment grade bonds.

Despite the financial improvement, it's important to check the financial strength of insurance companies before buying. The ratings can change monthly. Top ratings carry the following designations: A++ financial strength by A.M. Best; Triple A claims paying ratings by Standard & Poor's and Moody's; A and B financial strength ratings by Weiss Research.

Companies that carry A++ ratings from Best and Triple A claims paying ratings from Standard & Poor's and Moody's as of January 1992 include: The Guardian, Guardian Insurance and Annuity Company, New York Life, New York Life Insurance and Annuity Corporation, Northwestern Mutual, State Farm Life Insurance Company, and Teachers Insurance and Annuity.

Weiss' safest and largest insurance companies include Prudential Insurance Company of America, rated B; Metropolitan Life Insurance Company, rated B+; New York Life Insurance Company, Rated A; Northwestern Mutual Life Insurance Company, rated A+; State Farm Life Insurance Company, rated A+; Hartford Life Insurance Company, rated A; and Principal Mutual Life Insurance Company, rated B.

Regulators Must Regulate and Insurance Companies Must Save More Money

To avert potential failure, IDS recommends that all state governments revise their regulations governing how insurance companies can invest, how much capital and surplus (money to cover losses) they must have. The states also must improve the quality of their regulatory practices.

The Role of State Guarantee Associations

What if your insurance company goes out of business? Do you lose all your money? The answer is probably not. As mentioned earlier, you have some backup—but you will have to settle for less return than you were promised when you bought your policy.

Guarantee associations are created and funded by insurance companies doing business in each state to cover the potential losses that can result if an insurer defaults. When an insurance company is on the edge of going under, the state regulators try to get a strong insurance company to take over the policies of the insolvent institution. If those efforts fail and the court liquidates the insurance company, the state guarantee association usually will pay off the full face amount of the death benefits.

All states have laws that protect policyholders against insolvency. Most have adopted the model set by the National Association of Insurance Commissioners in 1970, which limits guarantee association liability to $100,000 in cash value and $300,000 in all benefits (i.e., death benefits and cash together). Some states, however, haven't adopted the model. For instance, Mississippi covers $100,000 in cash value and $500,000 in combined benefits. Kansas limits coverage to $100,000 in cash and $200,000 in combined benefits.

It would be helpful if the states got together and created some uniform standards. After all, bureaucrats are people, too. They own life insurance like the rest of us. So it's in their best interest to do something. Let's hope that they don't wait to act until a crisis has occurred, in the normal pattern of most state governments.

You Get Your Money Eventually

Forty-seven states have resident-only coverage. That means when an insurance company, which is chartered to do business in the state of the resident who is a policyholder, fails, the resident is protected. Beneficiaries who live out of state are also covered. If the insurance company is not chartered to do business in your state of residence, you are not covered by your state's guarantee association. Residents of the following five states are protected if their insurance company fails and is headquartered in any state in the union:

Alabama
New Hampshire
New Mexico
South Carolina
Vermont

→ ACTION ITEM ←

Consider buying insurance from a company admitted to do business or that is domiciled in the state of New York. There are few federal rules governing insurance companies. The regulations are left up to each state. New York has the most stringent rules regulating insurance companies.

New York State Has the Best Laws

New York has had the most diligent insurance department in the country. In 1990, half of all full-time accredited actuaries working for all state insurance departments worked for the State of New York. New York also has a history of adopting consumer reforms before other states. In 1941, the state adopted laws to protect consumers from an insurance company that went bankrupt. In addition, New York was the first state to put limits on how much insurance companies can invest in junk bonds. Back in 1987, when junk bonds still looked like a good deal, the state limited insurance companies to keeping no more than 20 percent of their assets in such investments. Finally, New York places stricter limits on life insurance companies' expenses, sales growth, agents' compensation, and financial management.

ACTION ITEM

Check to see where the insurance company's headquarters are located. The biggest defaults have occurred in Texas, Indiana, Oklahoma, New Mexico, Florida, Illinois, Arizona, Louisiana, and Washington.

Evaluate the Financial Strength of the Company

Several independent third parties evaluate the financial strength and claims-paying ability of insurance companies. The financial analysis is complex. But the rating agencies look at the following important criteria before giving a company a good or bad rating:

- *Profitability.* How much money does the company make every year or how much does it lose? Insurance company profits equal the premiums it collects or what you pay plus what the company earns on its investments less the company's expenses and dividends it pays out to policyholders.

- *Money or Capital.* How much does the insurance company have socked away for a rainy day? An insurance company has to have capital to make good investments, pay policyholders' dividends, and, most importantly, to pay claims. A company with plenty of capital has a cushion against economic tough times. Insurance companies lose money too. If they make poor investments, the value of the assets drops. If they don't manage the company wisely, expenses can get out of control. If they come out with bad products or impractical products that pay too high a rate, they can lose money. Or if new business is off or they have underestimated how much they have to pay out in benefits, they can lose money.
- *Reserves and Surplus.* This is related to capital. State laws require that insurance companies create a "legal reserve." That means they have to set aside a percentage of their assets so they always have money on hand to pay future claims.

An insurance company's surplus is what is left after the firm sets aside reserves, money to pay dividends and to pay business expenses. The surplus represents the buildup of earnings after expenses and charges. That is the net earnings from profits. It is similar to a corporation's retained earnings.

The rating agencies look at the balance sheet and income and expense statements of an insurance company, then do financial tests to make sure they are safe and sound and can pay claims to policyholders. Despite all this, the ratings themselves may not be enough. The rating system you rely on should analyze such things as public and private financial statements to determine the company's ability to pay death benefits to beneficiaries.

WHERE YOU CAN GET INFORMATION

Here are the major sources of information on the financial condition of insurance companies: A.M. Best evaluates the overall financial strength of insurance companies; Standard & Poor's, Moody's, and Duff & Phelps rate the ability of insurance companies to pay claims.

In 1992, however, Best made its rating system more stringent. The expanded rating system now includes A++, B++, C++, D, E, and F. The double + mark is given to the financially strongest firms in each class of A, B, or C. Reports cost $2.50. (Write to A.M. Best, Ambest Road, Oldwick, NJ 08858.

- Standard & Poor's Insurance Rating Service rates 135 life insurance companies based on their claims-paying ability. Firms rated AAA are the best. The ratings are updated monthly. Individual reports cost $25. Write Standard & Poor's, 25 Broadway, New York, NY 10004.
- Moody's Investors Service rates 60 life insurance companies based on their ability to pay claims. Aaa is the best. Annual summaries of all firms rated cost $125. Write: Moody's, 99 Church Street, New York, NY 10007.
- Duff & Phelps rates the claims-paying ability of 70 insurance companies. AAA is the best. Write: Duff & Phelps, 55 East Montgomery Street, Chicago, IL 60603.

Here are a few other sources of information on insurance company safety if you want to look further into the financial strength of a company:

- For a list of troubled companies and healthy firms with A++ Best ratings and triple A claims-paying ratings, write to the *Insurance Forum,* P.O. Box 245, Department CD, Ellettsville, IN 47429.
- The National Association of Insurance Commissioners sells reports on firms that are considered risky. The report costs $50. Write: NAIC, 120 West 12th Street, Suite 1100, Kansas City, MO 64015.
- Weiss Research, an analytical firm, also conducts an analysis of insurance company finances. Write: 22000 North

Florida Mango Road, West Palm Beach, FL 33409. The strongest insurance companies carry an A+ rating by Weiss Research.

➤ ACTION ITEM ◄

If you don't have time to research the financial strength of an insurance company, you can call or write the rating agencies. Call Standard & Poor's at 212-208-1527 for free ratings on insurance firms. A.M. Best charges $2.50 a minute for its ratings. Call 900-420-0400. You can also get ratings from a new rating service. Call Weiss Research at 800-289-9222. Weiss will send you a one-page report on an insurance firm's safety rating for $15. You can get an 18-page report on a company for $45. Call Moody's at 212-553-0377 for free ratings. Call Duff & Phelps at 312-368-3157 for free ratings.

Table 3–1 shows the rating schemes used by major rating agencies.

PUTTING IT TOGETHER

What kind of insurance company do you want? Throw out those firms that pay excessively high yields. If the rates are better than those offered by anyone else, the insurance company is taking big investment risks. You might live to regret that double-digit universal life policy or annuity you bought.

What you want first are firms rated A+ by A.M. Best. Then you want firms that are rated double or triple A in claims-paying ability by Standard & Poor's, Moody's, and Duff & Phelps.

Table 3–1
Table of Ratings

Agency	*Rating*	*Level of Risk*
A.M. Best	A++ to A+	Superior financial condition
	A to A−	Excellent financial condition
	B++ to B+	Very good financial condition
	B to B−	Good financial condition
	C++ to C+	Fair financial condition
	C to C−	Marginal financial condition
	F	In liquidation
Standard & Poor's	AAA	Superior claims-paying ability
	AA	Excellent claims-paying ability
	A	Good claims-paying ability
	BBB	Fair claims-paying ability
	BB	Adequate claims-paying ability
	B or less	Speculative claims-paying ability
Moody's	Aaa	Exceptional claims-paying ability
	Aa	Excellent claims-paying ability
	A	Good claims-paying ability
	Baa	Adequate claims-paying ability
	Ba	Questionable claims-paying ability
	B or less	Poor claims-paying ability
Duff & Phelps	AAA	Highest claims-paying ability
	AA	Very high claims-paying ability
	A	Average claims-paying ability
	BBB	Below average claims-paying ability
	BB	Uncertain claims-paying ability
	B	Risky claims-paying ability

It won't hurt you to pick out a firm with an A+ Best rating that has AA, Aa or AA claims-paying ratings. The companies rated double A are considered to be excellent or very high in financial condition and claims-paying ability. In addition, many of these companies pay higher dividends to their policyholders at the end of the policy year.

DROPPING DOWN IN CLASS CAN BE PROFITABLE

By dropping down just a tad from the AAA claims-paying companies, you might be able to get an attractively priced policy from a company that has a strong history of paying dividends.

Remember what dividends are? Dividends are excess profits that are returned to policyholders at the end of the year. In addition to being taken in cash, those dividends can be used to buy more insurance, help pay existing premiums, or reinvest in cash. Dividends are tax-free because the IRS considers them a return of a part of your premium.

So if you drop down in class in claims-paying ratings slightly, you can pick up some good deals from some firms rated A+ by Best. These will be companies that have historically paid out more in dividends over the past decade than other firms. At the time of this writing, the firms were rated double A in claims-paying ability. To Standard & Poor's, that means "insurers rated AA offer excellent financial security, and their capacity to meet policyholder obligations differs only in a small degree from insurers rated AAA."

Based on a statistical study published in *Best Review* in August 1990, several of these firms, with $100 million in net premiums written, distributed the most dividends at the lowest cost over 10 years. That assumes the dividends were invested at 5 percent interest rate after taxes and after the insurance company costs were taken out.

The data were based on a $50,000 whole life policy from a participating insurance company (that's one that pays you

Wealth Building Worksheet

Checking Out Insurance Companies

Before you buy, do a safety check on your insurance company. Then compare prices. If the company isn't the safest, don't invest. Check off the following:

1. A.M. Best rating ________
2. Claims-paying rating
   Standard & Poor's ________
   Moody's ________
   Duff & Phelps ________
3. Size of company
   Assets ________
   Premiums outstanding ________
4. Danger signals
   Are junk bond holdings greater than 14 percent of bond assets? ________
   Are junk bonds more than 20 percent of total assets? ________
5. Insurance company's bond rating
   Standard & Poor's ________
   Moody's ________
6. Compare how the insurance company invests its assets in relation to the industry average.

	Industry Average (%)	Potential Company
Government securities	13.7	________
Bonds	41.4	________
Stocks	9.7	________
Mortgages	19.5	________
Real estate	3.1	________
Policy loans	4.4	________
Miscellaneous assets	8.2	________

dividends) and assumes that the policy was paid up at age 100 or 85. Level premium payments were assumed to have been made, or modified payments were made only during the first 5 years of the policy. Thirty-six companies were surveyed.

FIRMS THAT PAY THE MOST DIVIDENDS AT THE LOWEST COST

Phoenix Life Insurance Company has an A+ Best's rating and Aa1 and AA+ claims-paying ratings by Standard & Poor's and Moody's. During the past 10 years, the firm ranked number one in dividend history assuming the dividends earned 5 percent interest after taxes annually over the 10-year period.

New England Mutual was ranked second. The firm also has an A+ Best's rating and a double-A claims-paying rating from Standard & Poor's, Moody's, and Duff & Phelps. New England ranked second if the dividends were taken out and reinvested annually at an after-tax rate of 5 percent annually over 10 years.

Connecticut Mutual also carries an A+ rating from Best and double-A claims-paying ratings from Standard & Poor's and Moody's. This firm ranked fourth in dividends paid out over the decade, if the dividends were reinvested at an annual after-tax rate of 5 percent over 10 years.

THE TOP 30

Table 3–2 lists the largest insurance companies—ranked by the amount of premiums outstanding—that meet the following criteria: They have been rated A++ by A.M. Best in 1992.

POINTS TO REMEMBER

- Shop carefully for an insurance company and a financial planner.
- Check the A.M. Best rating on the insurance company. An A+ rating means the insurance company is in strong

financial shape. Triple A claims-paying ratings by Standard & Poor's, Moody's, and Duff & Phelps indicate superior ability to pay on claims.

- Insurance agents with designations of CLU tell you the person has extensive professional training in life insurance. The ChFC and CFP designations tell you the financial professional has extensive training in all aspects of financial planning including insurance, taxation, investments, and estate planning.
- Beware of insurance companies that promise to pay excessively high yields on the cash value of whole life or interest-sensitive life insurance policies.
- Your state's guarantee association has funds to protect your death benefits and cash value if your insurance company goes bankrupt.
- Before you buy insurance, ask your financial planner to explain to you about the safety of your insurance company.
- Fee-only financial planners charge you a flat rate for their services. Some financial planners don't charge you for a financial plan, but they get paid a commission for the products they sell. Other financial planners charge a combination of fees and commissions.
- You can check the status of your financial planner by writing two professional organizations: the Institute for Certified Financial Planning, 7600 East Eastman Avenue, Suite 310, Denver, CO 80231; or the International Association for Financial Planning, 2 Concourse Parkway, Suite 800, Atlanta, GA 30328.
- If you do business with a financial planner who also manages money, ask to see the planner's financial statement that he or she filed with the Securities & Exchange Commission. This report tells you about the financial shape and investment experience of the money manager.
- Have your financial planner review your insurance and investment goals at least once a year.

Table 3–2
A++ Rated Insurance Companies in 1992

Company Name	*State*	*1992 Rating*
Aetna Life & Ann	CT	A++
Aid Assn For Luth	WI	A++
Allstate Life	IL	A++
Allstate Life of	NY	A++e
Amer Franklin	IL	A++e
Amer Genl L & A	TN	A++
Amer Genl Life	TX	A++
Amer Natl Ins	TX	A++
Amer Natl Life	TX	A++e
Canada Life Amer	MI	A++e
Canada Life Assur	CN	A++
Conn General Life	CT	A++
Contin Assurance	IL	A++p
Criterion Life	MD	A++e
First Colony	VA	A++
Franklin Life	IL	A++
Glenbrook L&A	IN	A++r
Glenbrook Life	OK	A++r
Globe L & A	DE	A++
Great West the of	CN	A++
Guardian Ins. & Ann	DE	A++
Guardian Life	NY	A++
Hartford Life	CT	A++
I T T Life Ins	WI	A++r
Jefferson-Pilot	NC	A++
John Hancock Life	MA	A++
John Hancock Var	MA	A++
Knights of Colum	CT	A++

Source: A.M. Best Company.

e stands for rating assigned to the parent company of a domestic subsidiary in which ownership exceeds 50 percent.

p stands for pooled rating or the rating assigned to companies under common management or ownership which pool 100 percent of their business.

r stands for the reinsurance rating.

Table 3–2 *(Continued)*

Company Name	*State*	*1992 Rating*
Liberty Natl	AL	A++
Lincoln Benefit	NE	A++r
Lutheran Bro Var	MN	A++e
Lutheran Brother	MN	A++
M M L Bay State	MO	A++e
M M L Pension Ins	DE	A++
Manufacturers L	CN	A++
Manufacturers L	PA	A++e
Manufacturers USA	ME	A++e
Mass Mutual Life	MA	A++
Metropolitan Life	NY	A++
Metropolitan Tow	DE	A++e
Minn Mutual Life	MN	A++
New York L & Ann	DE	A++
New York Life	NY	A++
Northbrook Life	IL	A++r
Northwestern Mut	WI	A++
Principal Mutal	IA	A++
Principal Natl	IA	A++
Pruco Life Ins Co	AZ	A++e
Pruco Life Ins Co	NJ	A++e
Prudential Ins	NJ	A++
State Farm L&A	IL	A++
State Farm Life	IL	A++
Sun Life Ins Ann	NY	A++e
Sun Life Ins Co	CN	A++
Sun Life of CN US	DE	A++e
Surety Life	UT	A++r
Teachers Ins & Ann	NY	A++
U S A A Life	TX	A++
United Investors	MO	A++
Valley Forge Life	PA	A++p
Variable Annuity	TX	A++
Western & Souther	OH	A++
Western-Southern	OH	A++e

4

How Much Should You Pay?

In some ways, life insurance salespeople are like lawyers: They have an answer for everything. They can't dispute your claim that you can get a better return in a common stock fund than a cash value life insurance policy, but they'll be happy to show you a chart illustrating how the tax-free return on your cash value is better than taxable investments.

Say you are in the 28 percent tax bracket and the insurance agent shows you an illustration with your cash value growing at 7.5 percent annually. That translates into a taxable equivalent yield of 10.42 percent. That's more than you could earn in bonds and about the same as the historical return on stocks, which are riskier over the short term. That sounds great. But as James Hunt, spokesperson for the National Insurance Consumers Organization (NICO), of Arlington, VA, says, "What you see isn't always what you get when you buy life insurance." That's because you pay hefty fees for life insurance; it costs money to get insurance protection. And (unless the insurance company does business in New York) many of the charges are not disclosed.

→ ACTION ITEM ←

Shop around and find a policy that costs the least. You want solid growth on your investment after commissions, fees, and other expenses have been deducted from your premium payments. You want the best returns over the long term.

Here are some guidelines, issued by NICO, to protect you from paying excessive fees and commissions on cash value policies:

- A first-year commission can be as high as 55 percent of your premium. Over the next two or three years, the commission is about 5 percent. After that, it averages about 2 percent.
- Policy fees should be about $40.
- Mortality fees range from 50 cents per $1,000 of coverage at age 10 to $200 per $1,000 of coverage for a person over 90 years old. These fees vary widely.
- Surrender charges or the amount of money you get back less the back-end load when you cash out your policy can be as high as 100 percent in the first year or drop to zero over 10 years. Surrender charges vary from policy to policy.
- Administrative charges range from $30 to $60 a year.
- State premium taxes are about 2 percent of your payments.

HOW CAN YOU TELL WHETHER YOU ARE GETTING A GOOD DEAL?

When asked how you can tell whether you are getting a square deal from the insurance company, NICO offered the following advice:

- Refuse to accept a cash value policy if the first-year surrender value of the policy is zero. The fees and commissions are too high. Insurance companies vary the mix of fees and commissions, but in the first year, the surrender value should be 50 percent of the premium.

- To make sure you are getting the best policy for the lowest price, get a quote from USAA Life, San Antonio, TX (800-531-8000) or Ameritus Life, Miami, FL (800-255-9678). Both insurance companies are low-cost providers. They do not employ insurance agents. They do not have a network for agencies across the country. You buy the insurance directly from the company. As a result, you don't pay a front-end load or sales commission for their products.

WHAT YOU SHOULD PAY FOR TERM INSURANCE

Initially, term insurance costs less than cash value insurance. But commissions, mortality fees, and other expenses are deducted from your premium payments. On average, a male nonsmoker, age 40, should pay about $165 to $200 in first-year premiums on $100,000 of term insurance. At age 45, he should pay about $205 to $240; a 50-year-old should pay between $320 and $355; and at age 60, the cost will be $600 to $635.

You can also cut costs by doing the following:

- Buy only as much insurance as you need to protect your family. Be sure to factor in your future income and inflation into the estimate of your insurance needs or you will shortchange yourself in the long run.
- Pay insurance premiums once a year, if you can afford to do it. It can cost you an extra $50 or more if you make monthly, quarterly, or semiannual payments instead of paying an annual lump-sum premium.
- A variable life insurance policy offered several years ago to the public illustrates how expenses can eat into the return on your cash value. The policy assumed a 12 percent rate of growth would be much less after expenses. During the first

five years, the policy averaged a negative 7.8 percent. After 10 years, the annual return increased to 4.6 percent; 20 years after the purchase, the investment averaged 8 percent a year.

Just as insurance companies are entitled to have profit margins, consumers are entitled to do business with the company that pays the best rates at the lowest cost with the best service and the potential to honor their commitments. That's why you have to take a good look at several policies. You will save a great deal of money over 20 years.

A WORD ABOUT NO-LOAD LIFE INSURANCE

No-load life insurance is one of the newest breeds of insurance products to hit the market. These policies claim to have no up-front sales commissions, but some experts say they're no bargain. For some agents, face amounts, and underwriting categories, traditional policies actually may be cheaper.

Here's the catch: A fistful of companies have come out with policies that have no sales commissions, renewal fees, or surrender fees. American Life of New York has a universal and single-premium product. Bankers Life of Nebraska, Lincoln, NE, peddles a whole life policy; Bankers National, Parsippany, NJ, sells renewal term and universal policies; Lincoln Benefit, Lincoln, NE, has term and universal policies; and USAA Life, San Antonio, TX, sells a universal variable life.

The policies are available through fee-only financial planners. You don't pay a commission on the policy. You do, however, have to pay a planner for services. A one-time meeting with a planner could cost you $500 for a financial plan and insurance. In addition, no matter who procures your policy, you will have to pay administrative fees, state premium taxes, and mortality charges. Also, the no-load policies may not have the flexibility to convert to other types of policies or enable you to qualify for lower rates if you have your health reevaluated.

In most cases, no-load policies are good deals over a short period. But if you plan to hold your policy for more than 10 years, the compound interest on cash value policies works better in the load products. So shop around and compare load and no-load policies.

ACTION ITEM

Buy savings bank life insurance if you are looking for an inexpensive policy. Savings banks in the states of Massachusetts, Connecticut, and New York sell such insurance. Savings bank life insurance is low-cost insurance sold by banks directly to the public. There is no costly agent force to support. The savings are passed on to the policyholders.

If you are interested in learning how to price both load and no-load insurance policies, you can refer to the following:

- The July 1993 *Consumer Reports* rates a number of policies based on cost and return. Although this information is out of date, it provides some useful guidelines.
- *Best's Insurance Reports,* available at your local library, presents the financial performance of insurance companies.
- "An Agent's Guide to Universal Life" looks at a number of universal policies and what they cost. For a copy of this booklet, send $1.50 to 408 Olive Street, St. Louis, MO 63102.
- The *Life Insurance Buyers Guide* is free; it is published by the National Association of Insurance Commissioners, 120 West 12th Street, Suite 1100, Kansas City, MO 64150.

- *Life Insurance: A Consumers Handbook,* by Joseph M. Belth, Indiana University Press, Bloomington, IN ($19.95) is an excellent primer on the ins and outs of life insurance.

  There are a couple of easy ways to compare term insurance coverage. Several rate quote services are available. You give the specifics of your term policy, and they will figure the one that costs the least for the best amount over coverage.
- Insurance Information (800-472-5800) is recommended by NICO. Five quotes cost $50. You also get the names and addresses of the companies.
- Select Quote (800-343-1985) covers 30 companies and will give you five quotes without charge.
- Insurance Quote (800-972-1104) gives you five free competitive quotes on 5 out of 50 companies. This service is also free.
- Life Quote (900-246-life) gives three free quotes.

ACTION ITEM

Ask the insurance quoting services what their relationship is with the companies they report on. Some insurance companies pay services to represent them.

SEVERAL INDEXES

Once you have several life insurance illustrations piled up on your desk, you can use the cost comparison index to find out which ones are the best deals.

There are many items to check when shopping for insurance. We'll get into that in a little more detail in Chapter 5, which talks about how to read and understand a life insurance illustration.

Here is a rundown of the cost comparison indexes to look at when you compare policies. If two policies cost about the same, do business with the firm that gives you the best service.

Rate-of-Return Index

The National Insurance Consumer Organization uses the rate-of-return index to compare policies. If you are interested in comparing policies, NICO will figure the rate of return on the policies less fees on the surrender value of your policy. It costs $30 for the analysis on the first policy and $20 for each additional policy. You can write NICO at 121 North Payne Street, Arlington, VA 22314, for more information.

The rate-of-return analysis tells you how much money you will have in your pocket when you surrender the policy. Based on the premium payments, NICO calculates what rate of return (interest rate) is needed to get the final surrender value of the policy. It tells you that you earned *x* percent on your premium payments because you received *x* amount of dollars back less expenses.

The math is complicated. All you need to know is that the higher the rate of return the better. It means you paid less in fees and other charges for the policy. So you had more money to invest. But keep in mind that the illustration you get from an insurance company is just a projection. Mortality rates, expenses, and interest rates change, so the insurance company will make those adjustments to your policy.

The NICO service is a good deal. It's worth it to spend a few dollars to find out which policy offers the best terms. NICO will give you a computer printout that compares buying a cash value policy with buying annual renewable term insurance and investing the difference in the premium paid at a 6 percent interest rate.

Comparing a policy to term and investing the difference will give you a good idea if you are earning enough on a cash value policy to make it attractive.

A word to the wise: If you have the discipline to buy term and invest the difference in fixed income or diversified stock funds, you can beat the returns on your fixed rate, cash value policies. Remember, however, that to do it, you must budget the money and put it away every year. Otherwise, buying term and investing the difference won't work.

What You See Isn't Always What You Get

Using NICO data in "Taking the Bite Out of Insurance," a handy booklet published by the nonprofit firm, say you meet the following assumptions:

You are age 40, don't smoke, and want a $100,000 universal life insurance policy. You will pay a premium of $683, and the agent gives you an illustration assuming a 9.25 percent interest rate.

NICO's analysis shows what you see from the agent and what you get after 5, 10, 15, and 20 years based on the cash surrender value of the policy. That's insurance lingo meaning you called your agent and told him you intend to cash out your policy because you want the money.

- The cash surrender value of your policy after 5 years is $864; you paid in a total of $3,415. The rate of return is −33.4 percent.
- The cash surrender value of your policy after 10 years is $4,756; you paid $6,830 in premiums. The rate of return is −1 percent.
- The cash surrender value of the policy after 15 years is $10,376; you paid $10,245. The rate of return is 4.3 percent.
- The cash surrender value of the policy after 20 years is $18,315; you paid in $13,666. The rate of return is 6.0 percent.

Cost Comparison Indexes

These numbers tell you what policy is cheaper per thousand dollars of coverage. You have to compare like policies, that is, term insurance to term insurance. You also have to compare the policies at the same age and with the same riders. Your insurance agent should provide you with commonly used indexes such as the interest-adjusted cost index, a method that's favored by *Consumer Digest*, a Chicago-based consumer magazine, as well as many financial advisors. This index is also know as the surrender cost index.

The interest-adjusted cost index looks at the time value of money of your premium payments, dividends, and cash value. In other words, how much was earned net of fees if, for example, you put your money in a bank savings account that earned 5 percent interest. The indexes look at when the dividends are paid and invested. The lower the index number, the better the policy or the less it cost per thousand dollars of coverage. And if you get a negative number, such as −1.0, it means the cash surrender value of your policy has increased more than 5 percent, the cost index rate used to determine the growth of your cash value and dividends.

A related measure that also looks at what your payments and dividends would earn, less fees at a 5 percent interest rate, is the net payment cost index. It goes hand in hand with the surrender cost index. It tells you what you pay per thousand dollars of coverage less fees.

WEALTH BUILDING PROFILE

Shop Around. Bill is reviewing a couple of cash value policies to find out which one is the best deal. He wants to purchase a $250,000 policy. Company A's whole life product has an interest-adjusted cost index of $1.43 after 20 years. Company B's policy has a cost index of $2.50. The $1.43 and $2.50 tell Bill what it would cost him for $1,000 of insurance per year over 20 years. But since he is looking for a $250,000 policy, he wants to see what it would cost for the entire amount. So he does some quick figuring by multiplying $1.43 times 250 times 20 to get $7,150. That's what Company A's $250,000 of insurance will cost him over 20 years. Company B's policy costs $2.50 times 250 times 20 or $12,500 over the same 20 years. As a result, Bill buys a policy from Company A.

Policies differ in cost and price at different ages: Look at the surrender and payment cost indexes over a time period. Some policies are cheaper the longer you own them. Since life insurance is supposed to be a long-term affair, it's best to see what the cost per thousand is over 10 and 20 years.

ACTION ITEM

Be patient. It takes a lot of homework to get the best insurance at the lowest cost. But if you save several hundred dollars, the savings can be invested for your retirement over the long term. For example, $200 a year placed in a tax-deferred investment at just 6 percent will grow to $7,800 over 20 years. You paid yourself a commission, rather than the insurance company.

Wealth Building Worksheet

Comparing Insurance Policies

Type of insurance: ______________

	Policy A	*Policy B*	*Policy C*
Amount of death benefits:	$_____	$_____	$_____
Amount of premium payments:	_____	_____	_____
Loads, Fees, Charges			
Up-front commission	_____	_____	_____
Mortality fee	_____	_____	_____
Administrative charges	_____	_____	_____
Policy fees	_____	_____	_____
State premium tax	_____	_____	_____
Cost or price indexes			
10-year interest adjusted	_____	_____	_____
20-year interest adjusted	_____	_____	_____
10-year surrender cost	_____	_____	_____
20-year surrender cost	_____	_____	_____

POINTS TO REMEMBER

- Shop around before you buy life insurance. Be sure to compare the premiums you pay for the coverage you want.
- Ask your agent or financial planner about the fees and commissions you will pay for the coverage.
- Compare the death benefits you will receive from several policies.
- Check the cash surrender values after 5, 10, 15, 20, and at least 25 years.
- Check the cash value based on the insurance companies' guarantee rates over 5 through 25 years.
- Ask your financial planner or agent for the internal rate of return on the cash surrender value of your policy.
- Compare the cost per thousand dollars of insurance by reviewing the surrender cost and interest-adjusted cost indexes list of several policies. The lower the cost index numbers, the cheaper the cost of the insurance coverage.

5

A Picture of Your Insurance

Buying life insurance is a lot like buying a car—you need to kick the tires and check under the hood before you sign on the dotted line.

Financial planners stress that you must take a close look at a life insurance policy's illustration. The illustration, or ledger statement, is a computer printout that shows you all the financial details of your insurance policy. It shows how much you have to pay for a specific amount of death benefits. If you have a whole, universal, or variable policy, you see the annual worth of your cash value and dividends.

Illustrations differ in form and style from company to company. But there are common elements to each company's report.

The first page of the illustration shows the following:

- Name of the company.
- The name of the person who is buying the insurance.
- The date of the illustration.
- Information about you: your age; your status of insurance, such as a nonsmoker or preferred; the type of policy (term, whole life, variable life); riders such as a disability waiver of premium.

- The amount of insurance or the face amount.
- The initial annual premium.
- What dividend option you have selected if you are buying a participating policy.

Subsequent pages of the illustration show:

- Several rows and columns of numbers listing the following items: policy years; annual premium payments; annual dividends, cash values, and premium payments less any dividends.
- A summary statement that includes the total premium payments, surrender values, and death benefits.
- Cost index information for 5, 10, and 20 years. Several different indexes may appear on the illustration.

The two most frequently used indexes are the interest-adjusted net cost index and the interest-adjusted payment index. The interest-adjusted net cost index is also called the surrender cost index (see Chapter 4). The indexes show you the cost of your policy per thousand dollars of coverage. The lower the number the better.

It's even better if you get an internal rate of return figure (IRR) on the surrender value of your policy and on death. The IRR is the percentage the investment grows over time assuming you made annual premium payments over the life of your policy.

The footnotes on the last page of the illustration explain assumptions that have been made about the growth of dividends.

The explanation page includes information about the policy loan rate, the cost indexes, and a tax statement.

SAMPLE ILLUSTRATION—TERM INSURANCE

Assume we are doing business with a financial planner who is showing us illustrations of term, whole life, and universal life issued by the A+ Insurance Company. The insuree for term insurance is J.J. Doe, age 35. J.J. does not smoke and gets a preferred rating by the company. The illustration assumes $100,000 of coverage with the disability rider known as a waiver of premium: If J.J. becomes disabled and can't pay his insurance premiums, the insurance company waives the premiums. The policyholder does not have to pay.

Table 5–1 shows us that the A+ Insurance Company's illustration for J.J. Doe, age 35, is for $100,000 of coverage. The insurance status is preferred. That means Mr. Doe is a nonsmoker. Otherwise his status could have been "rated." That means he would pay higher rates due to medical or occupational reasons.

You will also see that J.J. can convert this term policy to a cash value product to age 65. J.J. can also apply for reentry. This means he can take a medical exam and have his application reviewed by an underwriter. If he is in good health, he may qualify to pay lower premiums than other people his own age.

J.J. will pay a first-year premium of $130. The November 1, 1991, date means that the illustration numbers reflect that time period. They could be subject to change.

Now move down to the premium payment schedule. This illustration covers 20 years. You can see that J.J. pays higher premiums every year for his $100,000 term life insurance policy. In year 2, it cost him $142 for insurance. By year 5, when he was 39 years of age, it cost $186. During the first 5 years of the policy, he paid in a total of $789 in premiums for his coverage.

Look at year 11. J.J. is 45 years old. He applied for reissue or reentry. He is in good physical condition, and the company dropped his premium payments to $165. That's much less than the guaranteed maximum rate listed in the third column of the illustration. The insurance company could charge up to $642, the maximum allowable by law.

By the time J.J. is 54, it will cost him $645 a year for coverage. Over 20 years, the insurance will cost $5,494.

This example uses annually renewal term. But J.J. can get level term. He gets the same $100,000 coverage but pays level

Table 5–1
Term Insurance Example

The A+ Insurance Company
Insured: J.J. Doe November 1, 1991
Agent: Smith

Male, age 35, Nonsmoker Term
Waiver of Premium Benefit

$100,000 Annually Renewable Term, renewable to age 100 and convertible to age 65. Reentry to age 70.

First-year premium $130

Premium Payment Schedule

Year	*Age*	*Premium*	*Guaranteed Maximum*
1	35	$ 130	
2	36	142	
3	37	158	
4	38	173	
5	39	186	
	Total	789	
6	40	202	
7	41	217	513
8	42	236	541
9	43	252	573
10	44	276	607
	Total	1,972	3,225
11	45	165	642
12	46	204	675
13	47	235	709
14	48	255	752
15	49	275	809
	Total	3,106	6,812
16	50	338	887
17	51	401	990
18	52	465	1,114
19	53	539	1,255
20	54	645	1,409
	Total	5,495	12,467

Table 5–1 ***(Continued)***

The current premiums are guaranteed for the first six policy years. After the guarantee period, the current premium may be more or less than that shown, but will not exceed the guaranteed maximum premium. Any change will be due to reevaluation by the company of future expectations and will not be increased without prior justification to state insurance departments. Current guaranteed maximum rates include policy fees.

Reentry

The reentry rates illustrated assume receipt of satisfactory evidence of insurability prior to 10th and 20th policy anniversary.

Convertibility

The coverage is convertible without evidence of insurability to the age shown on page one of this illustration to most cash value plans of insurance with similar underwriting requirements.

Statement on Rounding

All calculations are performed in dollars and are rounded to the nearest dollar.

Cost Indexes

Net payment/surrender cost indexes per $1,000 based on current premiums with reentry:

10 year	1.91
20 year	2.45

Current premiums without reentry:

10 year	1.91
20 year	3.50

Guaranteed premium:

10 year	2.98
20 year	5.25

* Reentry assumes underwriting requirements are met.

This illustration is not a contract or part of a contract.

premiums for 5 or 10 years. The payments stay the same for 5 or 10 years; then the cost goes up for each successive 5- or 10-year period.

You may see term policies that pay dividends. There would be more columns in the illustration of a dividend-paying term policy. You may see columns that list the following:

- The insurance company's estimate of annual dividends to be distributed to policyholders.
- The potential reduction of premium payments through the use of dividends. The column would say net premiums for the year.
- The potential growth of dividends if invested to earn interest. This column is called accumulated dividends.
- The total death benefit by adding the accumulated dividends to the death benefit.

They Even Explain Things To You

The explanation section of the illustration states that the insurance company will guarantee it won't change the premium payments or the renewable term will not change years. After the 6th year, this particular insurance company can change the premiums that J.J. is required to pay. If the insurance company's earnings are down and the amount of claims paid out are up, the insurance company could require him to pay a higher premium. But the company is limited by law to a guaranteed maximum amount. Before it changes the premiums, the company also has to get approval from the state insurance commissions.

J.J. can apply for reentry rates before year 10 and 20 of the policy. That means he could be paying lower premiums if he is in good health.

The footnotes also say that J.J. can convert the policy to a cash value product without evidence of insurability. He doesn't have to take another physical examination.

Finally, the cost indexes are listed. This enables J.J. to compare the cost of this policy with others. The lower the index number, the lower the cost per $1,000 of coverage. To compare policies, however, you have to use the same policy feature for each product, in this case, an annually renewable term of $100,000 for a 35-year-old male nonsmoker.

A statement at the end of the illustration shows the loan rate, in this case, a variable loan rate of 9.8 percent meaning that the rate can change if interest rates change. In addition, the illustration states: "This illustration is not a contract or part of a contract." This means the illustration is just an example. In real life, there could be changes in the premiums you pay or the cash value buildup, if you have a whole life insurance policy.

WHOLE LIFE HYPOTHETICAL EXAMPLE

Assume we are dealing with the same insurance company. P. Jones is a 43-year-old male who wants a $100,000 whole life policy.

A whole life illustration such as the one shown in Table 5–2 provides identifying information—the insurance company, the insuree, the age, date, the amount of the policy, and the initial annual premium to be paid. You may also see a notice of the waiver of premium rider if elected, and what the insured intends to do with the dividends. If you have selected any other riders on the policy, they will also be listed.

In this example, P. Jones, age 43, has preferred status and wants a $100,000 whole life policy. He elected the option of "paid up additions" (PUAs). That means the dividends buy more insurance. Each annual dividend buys a mini-insurance policy.

P. Jones also selected the vanishing premium option. This means he will make larger payments up front, which increases the cash value buildup earlier in the policy's life. As a result of the faster accumulation of cash values in the policy, there is a time when no more premium payments are required. Future premium payments are borrowed from the cash value.

Table 5–2
Whole Life Example

Insured:	P. Jones	Male Age 43 PREFERRED
Amount:	$100,000 Whole Life	
Total Premium:	$1,710	
Benefits:		
Dividend Option:	Paid-Up Additions (PUAS)	
Other:	Vanishing Premium Concept	

The Vanishing Premium Concept: This illustration assumes premiums will continue to be paid by dividends and surrender of PUAs after annual cash payments are discontinued. Dividends are not guaranteed, but depend upon investment earnings, mortality experience, the expenses of the company, and any outstanding policy loans. If dividends are less than projected, additional payments could be required to achieve the illustrated results.

Year	*Annual Premium*	*Projected Year-End Dividends*	*Guar. Cash Value*	*PUAs Cash Value*	*Total Cash Value*	*PUAs Death Value*	*Total Death Benefit*
1	1,710	280	254	280	534	1,013	102,013
2	1,710	291	1,956	597	2,553	2,086	102,068
3	1,710	362	3,699	1,016	4,715	3,422	103,422
4	1,710	434	5,485	1,545	7,030	5,023	105,023
5	1,710	508	7,353	2,197	9,550	6,894	106,894
6	1,710	585	9,265	2,986	12,251	[illegible],045	109,045
7	1,710	666	11,243	3,927	15,170	11,487	111,487
8	1,710	751	13,282	5,038	18,320	14,232	114,232
9	1,710	842	13,648	6,338	19,986	17,300	117,300
10	0	937	15,369	5,822	21,191	15,359	115,359
11	0	1,035	17,132	5,374	22,506	13,709	113,709
12	0	1,136	18,238	5,001	23,939	12,342	112,342
13	0	1,244	20,769	4,731	25,500	11,299	111,299
14	0	1,352	22,639	4,551	27,190	10,526	110,556
15	0	1,459	24,534	4,467	29,001	10,008	110,008
16	0	1,511	26,468	4,485	30,953	9,732	102,739
17	0	1,679	28,439	4,626	33,065	2,742	109,742
18	0	1,793	30,428	4,890	35,318	9,990	109,990
19	0	1,902	32,436	5,284	37,720	10,479	110,479
20	0	2,032	34,454	5,824	40,278	11,219	111,219

Table 5–2 *(Continued)*

Age	*Total Premiums*						
60	15,390	1,679	28,439	4,626	33,065	9,742	109,742
65	15,390	2,221	39,541	7,411	45,952	13,497	113,497
70	15,390	2,976	48,774	14,957	63,731	23,962	123,962
95	15,390	5,807	87,374	199,359	286,733	219,718	312,718

Summary of Premiums

$100,000 Whole Life	1,710.00	145.35
Total Premium**	1,710.00	145.35

The cost for each benefit is illustrated above. The Total Premium includes the charge for any additional benefits.

Policy Loans

You may borrow, at any time, an amount equal to the Guaranteed Cash Surrender Value at an annual 7.4% interest rate, payable in advance. Policyowners with outstanding loans may receive reduced dividends.

Indexes

State:	*10 Year*	*20 Year*
Surrender Cost Index	0.36	1.33
New Payment Cost Index	12.00	8.59

Assuming the insurance company projections are correct, P. Jones will not have to make another payment after the ninth policy year.

An explanation of the vanishing premium concept appears on the first page of this whole life illustration. It is followed by the table that shows you how the insurance works—the nitty gritty of the illustration.

Eight columns identify the components of the policy. Column 1 shows the policy year; column 2 shows the amount of the annual premium payments; and column 3 is the insurance company's projection of the dividends they will pay at year end.

Columns 4, 5, and 6 show the cash value. Column 4 is the value guaranteed by the insurance company over the policy years. Column 5 shows how much the cash value increases with dividend payments. Column 6 shows the total cash value of Columns 4 and 5 added together.

Columns 7 and 8 show the death benefits. Column 7 shows the extra amount of death benefits purchased with the dividends. Column 8 adds the extra death benefits to the original $100,000 death benefits.

P. Jones is looking at a vanishing premium policy. He will pay $1,710 in premiums every year for 9 years. That's it. At the end of the first year, he will collect about $280 in dividends, and the cash value is $254. A small amount was taken out for commissions, mortality fees, and expenses. The cash value of the paid-up additions is also $280, and the total cash value equals $534. The PUA death benefits equal $1,013 dollars. He has $100,000 in death benefits already plus the $1,013, which equals death benefits of $101,013.

Let's look at year 9. P. Jones has been paying $1,710 for 9 years now. The dividends he will collect in the 9th year equal $842. The guaranteed cash value has grown to $13,648, and the PUA cash value equals $6,338. That gives P. Jones a total cash value of $19,986. P. Jones's PUAs bought an extra $17,300 of death benefits over 9 years. The total death benefit coverage is now $117,300.

After year 9, the premiums will continue to be paid by the dividends. By the time P. Jones is 63, the total cash value of the policy is $40,278. The total death benefits are $111,219.

Following the schedule of costs and benefits, there is a summary statement showing the total premiums paid at ages 60, 65, 70, and 95. Also listed are the accumulated value of the dividends, cash value, and death benefits at the same ages.

In addition, this illustration summarizes the premiums paid annually or monthly for $100,000 of whole life, and it provides information about the policy loans. In this case, P. Jones can get a loan equal to the cash surrender value. The loan rate is 7.4 percent. The dividends payments may be cut if he has an outstanding loan. This is known as direct recognition.

Next you see the interest-adjusted cost indexes for 10 and 20 years. The surrender cost index for 10 years is .36, and for

20 years it is 1.33. The net payment cost index is 12 and 8.59 for 10 and 20 years respectively.

You use these indexes to compare the same type of policy illustrations from other companies. The lower the index, the better your return and the lower the cost.

FEATURES OF UNIVERSAL LIFE

Universal life (UL) is a slightly different insurance organism. You can make flexible premium payments or level payments. You can vary the amount you pay every year to fit your budget. But you must be careful about skipping or making a low premium payment. You have to have enough money in the insurance policy to cover the death benefits.

In a universal policy, the cash value grows at a variable rate. The projections of cash values in the illustrations are made with assumed rates over the long term.

Universal policies offer you a choice of death benefit options. If you choose option A, your beneficiaries would collect the face amount or total amount of death benefits you originally purchase. So if you bought a $200,000 UL policy, your beneficiaries would receive $200,000 when you die.

Under option A, as your cash value grows, the insurance death benefit decreases. When you die, part of the proceeds represents your cash value and part represents the insurance.

Under option B, your survivors get both the death benefits and the cash value. You get more death benefits with option B because your policy is purchasing a level amount of death benefits instead of a decreasing amount of death benefits as in option A.

Conversely, you generally have a higher cash surrender value with option A because you are buying less insurance every year and more money goes into the cash value.

In Chapter 8, you will see which type of UL policy is right for you. Right now, however, it's important to understand the UL illustration.

Most insurance companies want you to pay a level premium for universal for a couple of reasons. First, it's a disciplined way to pay for insurance. Second, you prevent the policy from lapsing. Otherwise, the policy could shut down because of insufficient payments. A policy lapses when the worth of the cash value is not enough to pay for the insurance company's expenses and risk charges.

Third, the Internal Revenue Service has established guidelines on premium payment levels. If you violate the rules, your policy may no longer be considered life insurance. Then you could end up paying taxes when you borrow or withdraw money from your life insurance.

Universal Hypothetical Example

Table 5–3 shows a universal illustration. We will assume we are dealing with the same insurance company. This time Mr. J.J. Doe is 43 years old and wants $100,000 of coverage. He will pay 100 months in premiums through age 65.

The first two columns of Table 5–3 show the policy year and annual premiums. In this example, P. Jones pays $100 a month or a total of $1,200 a year for 20 years.

ACTION ITEM

Go by the guaranteed rate illustrated in the UL policy when you are evaluating the insurance policy. Financial planners say it is safer to pay based on the guaranteed rate. Otherwise, you could be paying premiums based on high policy rates of return, when in fact, interest rates have declined. If rates drop too far and you have overestimated, you will have to kick in more premiums to keep the policy in force.

Since this is an interest-rate-sensitive policy, three sets of interest rate projections are listed. The first rate of 8.6 percent

Table 5–3
Universal Life Example

Statement of Policy Cost and Benefit Information

Insured: Male Age 43 Nonsmoker
Amount: $100,000.00 Universal Life Option A
Monthly Payment: $ 100.00 Additional Lump Sum Payment: $ 0.00

Values assume payments through age 65

		(2) Current (Based on 8.600%)		*(3) Assumed (Based on 7.500%)*		*(4) Guaranteed**	
Year	*(1) Annual Payments*	*Cash Surrender Values*	*Death Benefit*	*Cash Surrender Values*	*Death Benefit*	*Cash Surrender Values*	*Death Benefit*
1	$ 1,200	$ 935	$100,000	$ 930	$100,000	$ 810	$100,000
2	1,200	1,993	100,000	1,972	100,000	1,688	100,000
3	1,200	3,134	100,000	3,084	100,000	2,582	100,000
4	1,200	4,359	100,000	4,365	100,000	3,492	100,000
5	1,200	5,674	100,000	5,519	100,000	4,416	100,000
6	1,200	7,088	100,000	6,854	100,000	5,354	100,000
7	1,200	8,611	100,000	8,275	100,000	6,304	100,000
8	1,200	10,252	100,000	9,790	100,000	7,262	100,000
9	1,200	12,020	100,000	11,404	100,000	8,224	100,000
10	1,200	13,925	100,000	13,123	100,000	9,185	100,000
11	1,200	15,977	100,000	14,953	100,000	10,137	100,000
12	1,200	18,191	100,000	16,905	100,000	11,076	100,000
13	1,200	20,579	100,000	19,986	100,000	11,994	100,000
14	1,200	23,152	100,000	21,201	100,000	12,887	100,000
15	1,200	25,925	100,000	23,556	100,000	13,749	100,000
16	1,200	28,921	100,000	26,065	100,000	14,572	100,000
17	1,200	32,163	100,000	28,743	100,000	15,344	100,000
18	1,200	35,674	100,000	31,606	100,000	16,054	100,000
19	1,200	39,481	100,000	34,666	100,000	16,687	100,000
20	1,200	43,611	100,000	37,942	100,000	17,223	100,000
Age				*Total Payments*			
60	$20,400	$ 32,163	$100,000	$ 28,743	$100,000	$15,344	$100,000
65	26,400	52,988	100,000	45,216	100,000	17,911	100,000
70	26,400	77,689	100,000	61,393	100,000	9,117	100,000
95	26,400	596,449	602,414	347,724	351,201	0	0

Tax Guideline Payments:
Maximum Single: $19,886.42
Maximum Annual: 1,665.03
MEC Guideline: 4,431.00

Expenses: One time policy fee: $50
Monthly maintenance fee: $ 2.50
Administrative fee: 3% of all payments
Commissions: $0

* Based on the maximum cost of insurance and the minimum interest rate of 4 5% If the cash value of your policy ever dropped to zero, additional premium would be required to continue coverage.

is listed under the column heading "Current." That's the rate the insurance company is paying at the present time. The second rate, listed under the column heading "Assumed," is an estimated rate of 7.5 percent. The last column, "Guaranteed," is the company's guaranteed rate of 4.5 percent.

Under the column headings "Current," "Assumed," and "Guaranteed," you will see the cash surrender value and death benefits of the policy corresponding to each interest rate scenario.

Again, footnotes explain the interest rates used, what mortality fees are being assessed, and when the payments would not be enough to maintain the policy under the assumptions used in the illustration.

You always get a death benefit of $100,000 regardless of the rate paid on the cash value. But, the cash surrender value builds up faster at the current rate of 8.6 percent. After 10 years of annual payments of $1,200, the cash surrender value equals $13,925. That's the money you would collect from a cashed-out policy. After 20 years, the cash surrender value is $43,611.

You cannot be certain you will make 8.6 percent annually over the next 20 years. You might not make 7.5 percent either. What you earn depends on economic conditions and interest rates in the financial marketplace. After 10 years, the cash surrender value is $13,123 assuming an average rate of 7.5 percent. After 20 years, it's $37,942.

For sure, you will collect 4.5 percent. At 4.5 percent, your cash surrender value is $9,185 after 10 years and $17,223 after 20 years.

As you can see, the value of your accumulated cash is dependent on the level of interest rates, the risk of defaults and the performance of the insurance company's investment portfolio.

No matter how much the cash value earns, P. Jones knows the beneficiaries will get $100,000 of death benefits. And if P. Jones cashes out early, the money earns at least 4.5 percent a year.

At the end of the universal illustration, a summary table shows how much has been paid in premiums at ages 60 through 95. Also listed are the total cash surrender values and death benefits under each assumption.

Internal Revenue Requirements, Too

There are a few other items at the end of the table. The IRS puts limits on how much you can pay into a universal policy. In the past, some people dumped a large amount of money into the policy at once. They used the insurance as a tax shelter because the cash value isn't taxable. Then they borrowed money out of the policy at below-market rates.

The IRS says that isn't fair. To prevent people from using insurance as a tax dodge, the IRS places strict limits on the maximum amount that can be paid into a universal policy on an accumulated annual basis. The calculations can get complicated. Fortunately, your financial planner or agent's computer will tell you what is the correct way to pay.

Under tax guidelines, the maximum single amount you can pay into this policy is $19,886. The maximum annual amount you can put in is $1,665.03 over 20 years. And the maximum you can put in annually for 7 years under the modified endowment contract (MEC) guidelines is $4,431.

An MEC is the IRS term for an insurance policy that violates the tax laws. If you put more into a policy than is allowed by law, you are penalized with a 10 percent fine and pay ordinary income tax on your gains in the policy when you withdraw cash or borrow money from your policy.

The gain in the policy that is taxed is the amount of cash value that is greater than the total premiums you paid into the policy.

ACTION ITEM

Stick to the required premium payment schedule set up for you by your financial planner. Then you don't have to worry about paying any income taxes.

Consult your financial planner about the rules involving how much you can pay into your UL policy. Your planner or insurance agent will refer to the tax laws and set your policy up so you don't violate the Internal Revenue rules.

At the bottom of the illustration (Table 5–3), you will also see the expenses charged by the insurance company. Like other kinds of insurance, there is an explanation section included in the illustration. The insurance company states that the cash values reflect the cost of insurance, the interest rates are subject to change, which bonuses are to be paid to the policyholder, and information on borrowing from the policy. It also shows the interest-adjusted payment and cost index over 10 and 20 years for the policy.

VARIABLE LIFE ILLUSTRATION

Once you understand universal life, variable life is easy. Because a variable life policy is similar to a universal policy, a sample illustration is unnecessary here.

Here is what you get with a variable life insurance illustration.

- Columns that list the year, your age, and three hypothetical investment returns. The Securities & Exchange Commission requires that you see two or more hypothetical returns. One assumes a zero percent rate of growth; the others show some expected return on your investment. You may also see another column with the current returns. You invest various subaccounts of types of common stock and bond funds when you own a variable life insurance policy. Since you own securities, the insurance industry must follow the rules of the Securities & Exchange Commission. The insurance company is required by law to segregate the premiums paid on variable policies into a separate account. The separate account is not subject to the insurance company creditors' claims. Because stock and bond prices fluctuate, investors must review illustrations with different annual rates of return to get an idea what they can earn and what seems to be a realistic return.

The illustration shows the annual premium, and under each hypothetical return, columns show the cash value, the surrender value, and the death benefits.

There are also footnotes and cost indexes and summary tables as in the other illustrations.

Juicing Up the Illustrations—Deception

Insurance is a numbers assumption game. By playing with assumptions involving expenses, cash value rates of return, dividend distribution rates, and other little items, you can make illustrations look rosier than they should be.

It's easy to make numbers say what you want by just pressing a couple of keys on the computer. An unethical insurance agent can fiddle with the numbers to make mediocre but reasonable cash values look terrific.

Most financial planners and insurance agents want your business. They want to build up a good reputation in the community. If they do a good job for people, the word gets around town and new clients come knocking at the door.

But there are always a few bad apples in every bushel. The manipulation of numbers can make a conservative illustration look like the deal of the century.

Boosting the rate of return on the insurance policy is one way to get attractive cash values in a short time. You get some amazing cash values over 30 years (see Table 5–4). Just by boosting the rates to 8 percent from 7 percent, $10,000 of accumulated cash value would earn an extra $2,100 over 10 years. If the money earns 1.5 percent more, or 8.5 percent instead of 7 percent, the cash value earns an extra $3,230 in 10 years.

Manipulating the Numbers

Just remember what you see isn't always what you get. The computer created those illustrated values. In reality, the

Table 5–4
Yields Make a Difference: How Much Extra You Make When You Boost Your Rate Assuming You Invest $10,000

Yield Differential (%)	*Yield Advantage in Dollars over Time*			
	1 Year	*1 Years*	*5 Years*	*10 Years*
.50	$ 53	$357	$ 356	$1,024
.75	80	538	358	1,555
1.00	107	373	722	2,100
1.50	161	564	1,097	3,230
2.00	215	757	1,481	4,417

Source: Shearson Lehman Brothers Inc.

Note: Bond prices fluctuate with investment rates. A base rate of 7% was assumed to calculate the advantage of getting extra yields.

insurance company may charge more in expenses and mortality fees. If interest rates come down, the interest rate they earn on their invested money may be lower.

Be suspicious if banks are paying only 4 percent on a one-year certificate of deposit and the insurance company is promising a 10 percent return.

Reasonable Rates of Interest

Insurance company money managers diversify company investments to get the best returns with the least amount of risk on their portfolios. They don't keep 100 percent in any single security, issuer, or industry. They split up the investment pie among different bond issuers, both corporate and government, and among different maturities ranging from 3-month T-bills to 30-year bonds. Diversification helps reduce the risk of losses. By owning a large number of securities of different issues, they protect themselves in two ways.

- First, a default by a few issuers will generally not hurt the overall performance of the investment fund because a large number of issuers are owned.

- Second, different investment assets perform differently. Stock, bond, and real estate prices, for example, don't always move in the same direction. So gains in some assets will offset losses in other assets.

Here's how insurance companies have diversified by asset class in the past, according to the American Council of Life Insurance.

- Insurance companies have held about 10 percent of their assets in common and preferred stock over the past 20 years. During that time frame, stocks have grown at an annual rate of 10 percent assuming reinvestment of dividends and capital gains.
- Insurance companies also keep part of their investment in real estate. Over the past 20 years, real estate has represented about 3 percent of assets. Real estate has historically returned about 3 percent over the rate of inflation over the long term. Over the past 30 years, inflation has averaged about 5 percent. So real estate, though it has its ups and downs, on average has returned about 8 percent.

So what do we get by combining a forecast of interest rate with a diversified portfolio of securities?

Well, most insurance companies agree to pay you at least a 4.5 percent guaranteed rate. Historically, American Council of Life Insurance companies have registered about 7.7 percent annual returns before they pay policyholders.

With all the diversification and ups and downs in the financial markets, you are safe to assume that a policy that shows an illustration around 8 percent is a fair estimate for 20 to 30 years.

Be skeptical when you see illustrations with double-digit returns. You could earn 12 to 15 percent in one year, if you're lucky and the financial markets are on your side. But you could lose just as much or more. Then those 12 percent cash values might grow at a measly 6 percent.

Deceptive Ways to Boost Returns

Be suspicious if you see illustrated values that grow annually at double-digit rates. Look closely at returns of more than 10 percent.

There are ways to alter an illustration to make it look as if the cash values are worth much more money than they should be.

Armand de Palo, chief actuary and vice president of Guardian Life Insurance of America, New York, computed some sample illustrations that show how an insurance policy can be doctored to look more attractive.

The realistic illustration is for a male, age 45, who buys a $100,000 whole life policy. The insuree has preferred status, and dividends are used to buy more life insurance. The insurance company uses the 1980 Commissioners mortality rates to set its fees. The company bases its projections on all fees being deducted. The rate of return on the surrender value after 30 years less fees is 5.66 percent. That includes dividends, too.

The insuree pays annual premiums of $2,148 a year for 30 years for the realistic policy. His total payments are $64,400. For that money the insurance company projects the following:

- At the end of 30 years, the cash surrender value of the policy is $169,131.
- Death benefits equal $244,586.
- The second year's dividend is $73.

The surrender value is money you would get if you cashed out the policy and took the money. The money is made up of the guaranteed cash value, the cash value of the dividends left on deposit, the cash values of any riders, plus a refund of any unearned premiums and prorated dividends. From these, any policy loans are subtracted.

The total death benefits include the extra insurance purchased with the annual dividends.

An insurance firm can boost the return on the realistic policy in several ways.

In Version 1, the company cuts mortality assumptions and fees by 10 percent, by assuming that the people who buy this policy will live 10 percent longer than other people of the same age and underwriting class. When less money is taken out in fees, more money is invested. More dividends buy more insurance and more of that cash value is invested. The money in the account compounds faster.

Version 1 costs the same as the realistic policy, but the second year's dividend is $126, compared with $73 in the conservative policy.

The projected cash surrender value after 30 years will be $174,697.

The death benefits total $251,998 at age 74.

Version 2 holds back paying your cash value for two years in addition to cutting the mortality charge by 10 percent. That really puts some zip in the old policy values later on. In year 2, you collect $203 in dividends up from a measly $73 in the conservative policy.

Over time the money builds up faster. So by year 30, the cash surrender value is $181,336, and the death benefits are $262,767.

Version 3 cuts expense charges to new policyholders. The existing policyholders pay a greater part of the overhead. The mortality fee is also cut by 10 percent, and the insurance firm holds back on paying the cash value.

Look what has happened to the dividend in year 2. It's up to $248 from $73 in the conservative policy. Because of all the cost cutting, the cash surrender value of this policy after 30 years is $186,062. The total death benefits equal $269,061.

Version 4 assumes more people than normal cancel or let their insurance expire. That gives the insurance company more cash in their bank account. Not only that, Bad Apple says the company is going to reward good customers who keep the policy for 20 to 30 years by paying them extra dividends and bonuses. On top of that, the company cuts the mortality fee by 10 percent, as well as the expenses.

This also puts some extra zing into the cash value. The gains the insurance company made on those people that cash

Table 5–5
Juicing Up the Returns on Life Insurance

Method	*The Surrender Value (What your policy is worth if you cash it out)*	*The Death Benefit (What your family collects when you die)*
Realistic & Conservative*	$169,131	$244,586
Version 1. Cut Mortality fee by 10%.	174,697	251,988
Version 2. Fiddle with the cash value; lower in early years, more later. Cut mortality fee.	181,336	262,767
Version 3. Let established policyholders pay overhead. Cut expense to new group of customers; lower cash values and lower mortality fees.	186,062	269,061
Version 4. Provide bonus for being a good customer for 20 years; cut mortality fee, cut expenses; and pay lower cash values during early years.	199,483	276,386

Source: Guardian Life Insurance Company of America.

* Conservative policy based on $100,000 whole life for person age 45 of preferred status. Premium payments are $2,148 a year. Current mortality assumptions are used. Dividends are paid based on current history. Excess interest rate 5% all years (9% total interest credited). Fixed expense loading.

out early are paid to the policyholders between years 20 and 29. And a bonus is paid in year 30 of $31,800.

You are really going to make a bundle on this one. The cash surrender value in year 30 is now $199,483 and the total death benefits are $276,386.

Table 5–5 summarizes the preceding manipulations of cash values for life insurance.

THERE'S NO FREE LUNCH

There is no free lunch when it comes to insurance. So, if the illustration seems too good to be true, it probably is. Experts say that it is best to look for conservative assumptions.

"Illustrations are basically worthless for evaluating an insurer's future performance and what a policy will actually pay," emphasized Mr. de Palo. "Very often a financially weaker insurance company will use more optimistic assumptions to boost their illustrations. This is most problematic in universal life where there is more latitude to tinker with projections."

Mr. de Palo's advice: When comparing illustrations of several companies for the same coverage, look for conservative assumptions. If something looks too far out of line, you know someone juiced up the illustration.

POINTS TO REMEMBER

Here's a checklist to help compare life insurance policy illustrations.

- See if the policy pays dividends.
- See if you can make flexible payments or level payments.
- See how many years you must pay premiums. If dividends buy more insurance coverage, years you pay the premiums should decline.
- Check the minimum interest rate used to calculate the cash value over the years.
- Know whether the policy's loan rate is a fixed or variable rate. Also look to see if your dividend payments get cut if you borrow some money from your policy.
- Verify whether the dividends paid out in the illustration conform to the amount the company has actually paid out over the past few years.

- Check to see if you get a bonus payment from the insurance company if you keep the cash value-type policy over a number of years.
- Check your insurability status. You may pay less with some types of annually renewable term insurance if you get a medical exam.
- Check on the method the insurance company uses to figure the interest they pay you. Be sure the rate they pay is based on the insurance company's average earnings on its investment portfolio. It is almost important to know whether the rate is based on newly invested money.
- Check to see if your life insurance illustration reflects what happens when other people fail to pay their insurance premiums.
- Check the internal rate of return on the cash and surrender value of your policy.
- Investigate whether—and how much—the premiums or benefits change from year to year.
- Look at how the cash value builds up.
- Check the effective interest rate paid on the cash value and the surrender value at different years.

Term Insurance

*I*f you want life insurance but can't afford to pay a lot of money for the protection, term insurance may be the answer. Here's the trade-off: Term insurance costs much less than whole life insurance, but you are only covered for a specific time span such as a year, 5 years, or 10 years.

ACTION ITEM

Check the terms of your term insurance contract to be sure you know the maximum amount the insurance company can raise your premiums. Understanding the highest amount you could be paying for insurance will help you determine if you can afford the policy. You may have to compromise by buying a lower amount of insurance.

WHY BUY TERM INSURANCE?

In many cases, term insurance is cheapest during the years when you need income protection the most. For example, a 35-year-old nonsmoker would pay from $195 to $240 annually for $100,000 of term insurance. The same coverage for a whole life policy that accumulates cash value could cost $1,600 to $1,700 for the same period.

A renewable insurance policy is the best option because you have the choice of renewing your policy—without evidence of insurability—at the end of each term. That means you can keep your coverage without having to pass a physical examination at the end of each insured period.

Insurance agents and financial planners often say that low-cost term insurance is one of the best ways a young family can afford income protection. It's also an ideal way to cover outstanding debts such as a home mortgage or a small business loan; the death benefits can be used to pay off any outstanding debts.

ACTION ITEM

Compare the costs of both types of policies before you obtain coverage. Remember, term insurance gets more expensive as you get older because the risk of death increases with age. By contrast, a whole life policy has level premium payments throughout because the risk is factored in over a longer period.

"Anyone who has a temporary need for protection and doesn't have cash flow and is living on a tight budget should consider buying term insurance," stresses Jerold Bischoff, CLU and second vice president at the New England Life Insurance Company in Boston. "Term is attractive to younger families that can't afford the larger premiums paid for whole life insurance. Some people buy term to cover outstanding debts from starting a small business or, for example, to cover a first or second mortgage."

You Just Get Protection—No Cash

Understanding how term insurance works is easy. If you die during the time period (or term) you are insured, the insurer pays your beneficiaries. The policy itself has no cash value. In other words, when you surrender a term policy, you don't get anything. You no longer have insurance coverage, and you don't have any cash value.

By contrast, when you buy a whole life insurance policy, you can collect any money that's accumulated in the savings portion of the policy if you cash out (or surrender) the policy (less any surrender or back-end charges). You can also borrow against the cash value of your policy at low rates. (See Chapter 7 for a detailed discussion of whole life insurance.)

Later in this chapter, we will look at the ins and outs of term insurance and how you can find the policy that matches your financial condition. For now, let's look at a profile of someone who owns a term policy.

WEALTH BUILDING PROFILE

Couple Can't Afford Whole Life Insurance. Jack, age 30, and Christy, age 28, are married and need life insurance. The couple have two children, ages 6 and 3.

The family can't afford a big premium. So Jack bought a $400,000 yearly renewable term insurance because it is more affordable than whole life. The policy includes a waiver of premium rider (i.e., in the event he becomes disabled, he won't have to pay the premium). The policy costs $440 for the first policy year. If Jack decides to renew the policy next year, it will cost $460.

By contrast, the annual cost for a $400,000 participating whole life policy with a waiver of premium rider is $4,099 per year. However, after the first policy year, the whole life premiums begin to drop because dividends are used to pay part of the premiums. By the time Jack turned 39, the annual cost of the policy would be down to $2,531. His term insurance at the same age would be $628.

As Jack gets older, the term premium will outpace the whole life premium. At age 55, it will cost Jack $2,684 in premiums for the $400,000 of term insurance coverage. The whole life-type policy would not cost Jack anything by that age, because the dividends will more than pay for the premiums.

Each year, the cost of the term insurance goes up, but Jack liked the idea and flexibility of deciding whether to renew the policy. In addition, he could convert the policy into whole life once his income increased and the difference between the term and whole life premiums was smaller.

ACTION ITEM

Talk to your financial planner or insurance agent about whether you need and can afford disability insurance. In case you get injured on the job and can't work, a disability policy will pay you about 60 percent of your income until you can go back to work. If you are permanently disabled, you will be assured of income for your lifetime. When you buy a policy, be sure it is noncancellable. Once you sign on the dotted line, the insurance company can't cancel the policy as long as you pay on time. You should also be sure that you have the option to renew the policy every year and that the protection is indexed to the rate of inflation.

YEARLY RENEWABLE TERM VERSUS FIVE-YEAR RENEWABLE TERM

Term insurance is available for different periods. It may be renewable every year, or every 5 or 10 years. When you buy a 5- or 10-year renewable term policy, you lock into a lower initial rate compared with yearly renewable term insurance. However, over the long term, you end up paying more. For example, if Jack from the prior profile had purchased a 5-year renewable term policy, the premium would be $1,016 when he reached age 40 (the 11th policy year). The premium on the annual policy at that age is $700. At age 60, the premium is $3,556 for the annual policy compared with $7,340 for the 5-year term policy.

Do a policy-by-policy comparison of annually renewable and level term life insurance policies before you obtain coverage. Look at the total premiums you will have paid over the long term on the annually renewable and level term policies.

SHORT-TERM PROTECTION

Term insurance is a better deal than whole life for the short term. The reason: If you surrender your cash value policy during the initial policy years, you lose both your insurance coverage and the amount in the savings portion of the policy. Commissions, expenses, and mortality fees are deducted from the premium payments. It takes 11 years for the money to earn enough compound interest to equal the total amount of premium payments that are invested.

Again, let's use Jack as an example. If Jack opted to buy a whole life policy, by the end of the 11th policy year he would have paid a total of $35,157 in premiums and his cash value would be $36,892. If Jack surrendered his policy at that point, he would have bought $400,000 of coverage for 11 years and received $1,785 ($36,892 – $35,157) for doing so.

Now assume Jack bought the annually renewable term policy. At the end of the 11th year, his total premium payments would add up to $6,116. He would have paid $29,041 more for the whole life policy over the same time period. That's $29,041 more than he could afford for the whole life insurance policy. So, foregoing the $36,898 cash surrender value of the whole life policy is a small price to pay when you can save over $29,041 in payments. That's money Jack needed to support his family and pay the bills.

You Can Renew Your Term Policy with No Strings Attached

Many young wage-earning families prefer the cost and the flexibility of term insurance. Most term policies will let you renew until age 65 or 70. After that you may be out of luck. Consequently, term policyholders should talk to their insurance agent or financial planner periodically to determine whether a different type of coverage is needed.

You Might Be Able to Get a Price Break

Some term policies are revertible. That means you can reenter at a lower premium rate if you are in good health and pass another medical exam and evaluation by the underwriter (see Chapter 5, Table 5–1). It's rare to find revertible policies today. However, some insurance companies will reduce your premium if you take a new physical exam after a certain number of years. Insurance companies only do this if the actuaries—the people who calculate insurance statistics and figure out how to price and pay claims on policies—agree it is a good idea.

YOU ARE SOMEONE SPECIAL WHEN YOU BUY A NEW POLICY

Actuaries decide how to price a policy on the basis of the pool of people who are currently buying insurance. This pricing policy assumes that a healthy person who buys a new insurance policy is a better risk than someone the same age who bought a policy a long time ago. Many insurance companies base their rates on what they call attained age. Attained age is your age at the time you renew the policy. For example, if you are 38 when you renew your policy, your rate is the same as the rate for every other 38-year-old, regardless of when you bought your policy. There are some pluses and minuses to buying revertible policies.

On the plus side, the term insurance illustration in Chapter 5 shows that a 35-year-old nonsmoking male gets a price break at age 45 if he passes a medical examination. By the end of policy year 10, the insured paid $276 for $100,000 of annually renewable term insurance. But in policy year 11, our 45-year-old insuree pays $165 for the coverage. By policy year 15, he is paying $275 or virtually the same amount he paid in policy year 10 for the insurance coverage.

There are drawbacks, too. A 1986 *Consumer Reports* survey of several revertible insurance policies found that you have to shop far and wide to find a good deal. Based on the cost per thousand dollars of coverage, the survey found that revertible policies can be a gamble. If the policyholder becomes ill and does not pass the medical examination and qualify for the lower rate, the policies become very expensive.

ARE YOU A CONVERT?

What if you can afford a cash value policy after you've owned a term policy for several years? Most insurance companies will let you convert a term policy to whole life up to age 65 or 70 without evidence of insurability. This gives you the flexibility to switch as your needs change. For example:

- You can convert and take advantage of the built-in savings option with a cash value policy.
- After you've accumulated enough cash value, you can borrow money from the policy at attractive rates that may be lower than current bank charges.
- When you convert to a whole life policy, you have the option of locking into level premium payments for the remainder of the life of the policy.
- You can take advantage of the conversion feature to switch to a whole life policy without having to pass a medical exam. This can be important, especially if you are later diagnosed with a health problem.

TRICKY CONVERSION FEATURES

You almost have to have a PhD to figure out the nuances of term insurance. If you buy the wrong kind of contract, it's going to cost you money. Who wants to spend money to convert a term policy to whole life? That's what may happen if you do business with an insurance company that lets you convert a term policy to whole life based on original age pricing. Some insurance companies may require you to pay extra money at the time you convert based on the age at which you convert.

You also have to be wary of how your waiver of premium fits in with the conversion to a cash value policy. The best insurance companies will waive your premiums if you become disabled at the time that you convert your term policy to whole life. But some companies don't waive the premiums for the converted policy, or they require a waiting period before paying out the money.

After you've converted to whole life from term, you will accumulate cash value in the policy. Then you can borrow at attractive rates, possibly lower than the local bank rates. (You start building up cash value after you convert the term coverage to whole life, not before.)

How do I decide when it's time to convert my term insurance policy into a whole life policy?

You must answer several questions before you can make a decision:

- **Will your current cash flow accommodate the higher premiums needed for whole life?**
- **Will you still be able to meet your other long-term savings goals (e.g., children's education, your retirement)?**
- **Do you have adequate disability insurance coverage to provide you with enough income to live on if you get injured and can't work?**
- **What will your death benefit needs be in the future? Will there be cash to pay estate taxes if any are incurred?**
- **Are you planning to use the cash value of your policy in the future?**
- **Did you sit down with your agent and do an insurance needs analysis?**

What choices of coverage do I have if and when I convert my policy?

Before you buy term coverage, check to be sure the contract states what type of coverage you can get when you convert. Most companies enable you to switch to whole life, universal life, or variable life. If you switch to whole life you may make level premium payments. When you buy universal life you can vary your premium payments based on your financial condition.

Do I get a price break when I convert my term policy?

Yes and no. If you can convert your policy based on original age pricing, your premiums will be lower than if the converted policy is priced based on attained age. The original age policy is priced based on your age when you bought the term policy. For that reason, the policy is retroactive. That means you may have to fork over some money to put in the cash value of the converted policy.

If you convert your policy to a cash value policy based on attained age, you will not have to come up with extra money to make up the difference. However, your premium payments will be higher than a converted policy based on your original age.

I can afford term insurance, but I can't quite pay for a cash value policy. Is there some middle-of-the-road insurance product that provides me with both term and whole life insurance?

Yes. You might consider a whole life policy with a flexible term rider. This policy is cheaper than a traditional whole life policy and more expensive than a term policy. You decide on the amount of coverage you need and what you can afford to pay; the insurance company determines what proportion of term and whole life insurance fits the bill. In the early years of the policy, most of the coverage probably will be obtained through term insurance. As the years go by, the dividends you pay purchase more permanent coverage, and the term insurance is reduced. Eventually, 100 percent of your coverage is whole life insurance. The replacement process can be accelerated at any time by purchasing additional permanent coverage.

Flexible term riders can also be hooked onto variable and universal policies. Remember, the universal policy lets you make flexible premium payments. A variable life insurance policy enables you to invest the cash value in common stock and bond mutual funds. So the returns on your cash value will fluctuate in a variable life insurance policy.

You can also get a combination term and whole life policy with increasing insurance coverage. Thus the policy can serve as an inflation hedge. As the cost of living goes up, so does the income protection for the family.

Another alternative is to buy what is called a modified whole life insurance policy. With this type of policy, your payments are lower than normal in the early years of the policy and rise as you get older.

If you are considering buying a combination insurance policy, check the cost per thousand dollars of coverage and the interest-adjusted cost index. It might be cheaper to buy an annually renewable term. Also, look at the policy illustration to determine how long you have to wait before the cash value starts to build up.

OTHER KINDS OF TERM INSURANCE

Decreasing Term

Decreasing term insurance policies can be used for special circumstances such as paying off the debts of the insured. The death benefit attached to these policies declines to zero after a specific period, usually 10 to 20 years, or at age 65. You pay a level premium for the coverage. Decreasing term insurance can be very expensive.

Mortgage insurance is one common type of decreasing term policy. For example, suppose the family breadwinner dies one month after the family takes out a $200,000 mortgage on their home. The term of the note is 15 years. The insurer would pay off the entire balance of the mortgage, or $200,000. If the breadwinner dies during year 14 of the mortgage, the insured only has to pay the balance due—an amount unlikely to be more than a few thousand dollars. In effect, the amount of insurance could be just a hundred dollars, depending on the age of the insured and the principal that's been paid off on the house over the years.

Family Income Riders

This type of term insurance provides coverage for a surviving spouse for a specific period of time, generally between 10 and 20 years. In addition, extra insurance can be purchased when the insured has young children. The parent would buy a term rider on his or her policy that would cover the children. But some experts say that buying insurance for children is a waste of money. The chances are slim that a child will die unexpectedly. The coverage declines as the youngsters get older. If the insured lives beyond the number of years stated in the contract, the coverage expires.

Be careful. If you buy a decreasing policy such as a term to age 65, you could regret it if your health deteriorates. You won't want your coverage to drop when you know you have a heart problem. With annually renewable term, however, you can renew without evidence of insurability and know the amount of your coverage will stay the same over the years.

Can I get term insurance through my employer?

Most employers pay for at least a portion of the coverage. They buy low-cost group term insurance as an employee benefit. In many cases, the insurance is free as long as you continue working for the company. There is one caveat to employer term insurance. The cost of the term insurance up to $50,000 is not considered taxable income. The premium payments on employer term insurance over $50,000, however, are considered taxable income to the employee.

My uncle has an endowment policy that has been paying him income for over 15 years since he retired. Should I look into buying an endowment? How does it work? It sounds like a good deal—term insurance plus retirement income.

An endowment is an odd kind of insurance policy that used to be popular before Uncle Sam changed the tax laws in 1983. It works this way: The face amount or the amount of death benefits you purchase equal the cash value at the end of the contract period. If you die, for example, before you reach age 60, your beneficiaries collect the death benefits. However, if you outlive the policy, you have the value of the death benefits in cash, which can be used as a source of retirement income.

Endowments bought before 1984 are grandfathered in by the tax laws that have changed the tax status of this product. Insurance companies stopped issuing endowments that mature before age 95 because these policies were no longer considered life insurance policies but tax shelters.

If you are looking for an alternative to an endowment, you might consider term insurance and invest the premium difference in a retirement savings account. Or you might consider purchasing a universal or variable life insurance policy since part of your money buys insurance and part is invested in accounts that pay current rates of interest or that track the performance of the stock market.

I'm planning to buy a car. Should I get life insurance to cover the car loan?

Avoid credit life insurance. Don't let the lender talk you into paying for a small life insurance policy to cover the debt in the event of your untimely death. Credit life insurance, as it is known, remains one of the biggest consumer ripoffs in the country. Buyers are being overcharged as much as a billion dollars for insurance that covers installment debt.

According to a 1991 report by the National Association of Insurance Commissioners, only 39 percent or $975 million of the $2.5 billion in premiums collected for credit life sold to people by banks, finance companies, and auto lenders was used to pay claims.

In 1991, the Consumer Federation of America and the National Insurance Consumers Organization found that 43 percent of premiums were paid out in claims.

"Credit life insurance is still one of the worst insurance ripoffs," reports Stephen Brobeck, executive director of the Consumer Federation of America, a consumer group in Washington, DC. "Insurers should be paying out 70 percent of the premiums in claims. That level assures lenders a reasonable amount of profit without overcharging people."

Lenders take advantage of some buyers' ignorance about credit life and sell them high-priced policies. In the credit life insurance market, lenders do the shopping for the insurance. As a result, many lenders purchase insurance that pays them the highest commissions.

Overcharges are greater in some states than others, according to the Consumer Federation of America report. The most reasonably priced policies are sold in New England. Consumers are especially overcharged in the Southeastern states.

Wealth Building Worksheet

Term Insurance

Is term insurance right for you? If you answer yes to the following questions, buy term insurance.

- Is your income low but your insurance needs high?
- Do you need temporary coverage until you get your career off the ground and make more money?
- Do you have most of your money and assets tied up in a new business venture and need a lot of cheap coverage?
- Do you already have a cash value policy, but need some extra low-cost coverage for the family or because you have borrowed a lot of money? Do you have other short-term insurance needs?

Comparing Term Insurance Policies

		Policy A	*Policy B*	*Policy C*
▶ Amount of insurance		$_____	_____	_____
▶ Premiums to pay for renewable policy	Year 1	$_____	_____	_____
	Year 5	$_____	_____	_____
	Year 10	$_____	_____	_____
	Year 20	$_____	_____	_____
▶ Is the policy convertible?		_____	_____	_____
▶ Is the policy renewable?		_____	_____	_____
▶ Is there a guaranteed insurability rider?		_____	_____	_____
▶ Is the policy price on:				
select and ultimate tables?		_____	_____	_____
attained age?		_____	_____	_____
▶ Do I get a waiver of premium if I convert the policy at the time I am disabled?		_____	_____	_____
▶ Interest-adjusted net cost indexes over	5 years	_____	_____	_____
	10 years	_____	_____	_____
	20 years	_____	_____	_____

The best way to avoid being gypped by credit insurance lenders is not to buy their product. Remember, credit life insurance is an optional purchase. You are not required to obtain this kind of coverage when you purchase a big-ticket item on an installment plan. Most people are already protected by other life insurance policies or other assets if the borrower dies.

POINTS TO REMEMBER

- Term insurance is low-cost coverage for a short period of time.
- Remember that disability insurance coverage is extremely important, too. You want income protection in case you can't work due to illness or injury.
- Renewable term insurance is the best option because the choice of whether to continue coverage is yours. Annual renewal is cheaper than renewals at other time lapses.
- Renewable term insurance coverage can be renewed without evidence of insurability.
- You can convert your term insurance policy to whole life insurance without evidence of insurability up to age 65.
- You can buy a policy that is a combination of term and whole life insurance. The premiums will be about midway between a whole life and a term policy.
- Decreasing term insurance can be used to cover debts such as a home mortgage. Decreasing term is high-cost insurance compared with other types. It is low cost compared with paying off the loan on your own.
- Family income riders can be placed on your permanent coverage.
- Many employers offer their workers life insurance coverage as an employee benefit.
- Avoid credit life insurance.

7

Whole Life Insurance

Whole life insurance is as American as Mom and apple pie. According to the *1990 Life Insurance Fact Book,* despite the new products on the market, 35 percent of all life insurance sold is whole life. Why?

Richard Mesnick, CFP (Certified Financial Planner), Atlanta, GA, claims that the reason for this popularity is that many policyholders like the idea of permanent protection and the discipline of a forced savings plan.

STRAIGHT LIFE

Some advantages to straight life insurance are:

- The premiums stay the same every year.
- The interest on the policy's cash value accumulates tax-deferred.
- A savings feature is automatically included in the premium.
- The insurance company may pay dividends that can be used to purchase more insurance or to pay part of your premium.
- You get a relatively large amount of permanent protection for your premium dollars because the mortality fees and other costs are paid over the life of the contract.

- The death benefits stay the same unless you borrow against the cash value and don't pay back the loan. In that case, the death benefits will be reduced by the amount of the loan and accumulated debt interest.
- Your beneficiaries don't pay income tax on the death benefit proceeds. If the proceeds are paid out in the form of an annuity, part of the monthly payments is taxed as interest income. However, the money in the annuity grows tax deferred until distribution.
- The insurance policy can be used in estate planning. (Chapter 12 will discuss the use of life insurance in estate planning in more detail.)

ACTION ITEM

Consider buying a modified premium plan, if you are temporarily strapped for cash but want a whole life insurance policy. You could pay low premiums for five years. After that, your premiums might double. The advantage is that you get permanent protection that you can afford in your present financial situation. Another version lets you start out low and gradually pay higher premiums. After 20 years, your whole life premiums stay the same.

ACTION ITEM

Check with your insurance company to see if living benefits riders are permitted by your state insurance regulator. You can get living death benefits from many insurers. If you are terminally ill, you can collect somc of your death benefits before death to help pay your medical bills. The money can also be used to pay for a nursing home.

→ ACTION ITEM ←

Purchase a cost-of-living rider for your policy if you want your death benefits to increase with inflation. You can have your dividend buy more insurance, or you can buy a policy that tracks the Consumer Price Index.

→ ACTION ITEM ←

Purchase joint insurance if both spouses want coverage. Joint insurance can also be useful when one spouse is uninsurable. There are two types of joint policies. One pays off when the first spouse dies. The surviving spouse typically can then buy a new insurance policy. With a second-to-die policy, the insurance pays off when the second spouse dies. This type of policy is often used in estate planning.

WEALTH BUILDING PROFILE

Young Family Buys Extra Insurance with a Term Rider. Jack, age 30, has a terrific job. His wife is expecting a baby in a few months. Now Jack wants to buy more insurance. He has a policy at work, but that's not enough coverage. So he sat down with his insurance agent, who is also a financial planner, and they mapped out a plan to protect the family in the event of his unexpected death.

Jack likes the idea of straight life insurance. He prefers making annual premiums. He also likes the idea of using the dividends to buy extra insurance coverage over the years. That way, the death benefits would keep pace with inflation and his income.

He bought a policy with a total of $400,000 in coverage. The waiver of premium for disability costs him $54 a year.

And the term rider costs him $138 a year. His first-year total premiums were $2,205. That bought $200,000 in death benefits. The other $200,000 in coverage is paid for by the dividends. And by the time Jack reaches age 65, he will have a guaranteed cash value of $90,406. The total surrender value, if he wants the cash to use for his retirement, will equal $349,606. That's assuming the insurance company pays dividends and interest based on current rates over the next 36 years.

PAYMENT OPTIONS

If you don't want to pay premiums over the long term, other choices are available. If you make one payment, the policy is called a "single premium whole life" policy. If you pay for 20 years, it is called "20 pay life." If you decide you want your policy paid in full by the time you reach age 65, it's called "life paid up at 65." Naturally, the premium is higher for such policies.

On the plus side, your cash value grows faster tax-free. Consequently, you can borrow against the cash value long before you could with a straight whole life policy.

For example, let's assume a person age 35 buys a $100,000 policy that's paid up at age 65. The premiums are $1,607, or $592 a year more than a straight life policy. After 10 years the policyholder would have accumulated a cash value of $19,500. After 15 years, the cash value would grow to $60,000. By age 65, the cash value is $158,207. In contrast, a straight life policy cash value only grows to $10,100 after 10 years, to $20,613 after 15 years, and to $93,077 by the time the policyholder is 65.

NOW YOU SEE IT, NOW YOU DON'T

Many insurees are choosing whole life policies with vanishing premiums. The dividends are used to pay part of the premiums.

Here is how it works: A whole life policy can be set up so that the policyholder pays premiums for 5 to 10 years. The insurance company estimates that by the end of that time, the dividends and accumulated cash value are enough to pay your premiums for another three to four years until the policy is paid up.

For example, the same 35-year-old could put $1,607 into a $100,000 whole life policy that would be paid for after eight years. The eight-year period is determined by the insurance company based on its estimate of interest rates and the dividends it expects to pass onto the policyholders. In the first year, the policyholder starts with $100,000 of coverage. The policyholder is guaranteed that amount for as long as he or she keeps the policy. The annual dividends buy more insurance, or as the insurance agents call it, "paid up additions."

Every year you have more insurance coverage. That generates more dividends. By the 9th policy year, the death benefit guaranteed by the insurance company is $59,410, while the death benefit from the dividends equals $42,587. You bought a policy with a face amount of $100,000 of coverage. But your total coverage is more because of the dividends, which are used to purchase insurance. In this example, the total death benefit in year 9 equaled $102,174.

Once you reach this stage, you don't have to pay any more premiums. The dividends from all the insurance coverage you have accumulated should be enough to pay your premiums. Over time, the insurance policy will be paid off.

Although the policyholder pays no more premiums, the cash values are less in the vanishing premium policy compared with the policy that's paid for at age 65. For example, after 10 years, the cash value has accumulated to $14,642 or almost $5,000 less than the policy that's paid for at age 65. In 30 years, the cash value in the vanishing premium policy is almost $59,000. This is substantially less than the policy where premiums were paid for 30 years. Consequently, Mr. Mesnick recommends that policyholders evaluate their insurance needs before or after the vanishing period of their policy. If they need more insurance, he advises them to buy a different policy that will give them more cash value buildup.

Warning. With a vanishing premium policy, there is no guarantee that you will receive the dividends that were estimated to help pay off your policy based on the illustration. If mortality assumptions and the insurance company's earnings are lower than expected, your dividends could be lower. Policyholders may find themselves paying premiums for a longer time than they expected. As a rule of thumb, for every 1 percent drop in interest rates, add two years of premium payments.

INTEREST-SENSITIVE WHOLE LIFE

Interest-sensitive, current assumption whole life insurance may be the answer for policyholders who want to earn more than they would in a straight whole life policy that pays a guaranteed cash value plus dividends.

WEALTH BUILDING PROFILE ***Policy That's Paid Up at Age 65.*** Alex, age 35, just launched a new business after working for a corporation for 8 years. He has put off buying life insurance for a long time, but now he feels he needs some coverage. Alex took a pay cut when he started his business. However, he can afford to pay $1,511 in premiums for a $100,000 interest-sensitive whole life policy that will be paid up by age 65.

He likes the current policy rate of 8.25 percent. Although interest rates have been declining, Alex feels that over the long term he will earn more than with an ordinary whole life policy. By the time he's ready to retire at age 65, the cash value in the policy will have grown to $128,825.

Policyholders are required to pay level premiums on an interest-sensitive whole life policy. Universal life policies are born of interest-sensitive whole life insurance (see Chapter 8). There may be some flexibility when you buy an interest-sensitive policy. Lynn Hopewell, CFP, The Monitor Group, Inc., Falls Church, VA, says that some insurance companies let you choose between low-premium and high-premium versions of the policy. You can pay lower than normal whole life premiums, for example, for the first 5 policy years. Then the insurance company will make a redetermination. You could pay more for your policy based on the insurance company's estimates of interest rates and mortality. Another alternative is setting up a vanishing premium policy. The policy will be paid up after 9 to 10 years. It will remain paid up as long as the cash value you have accumulated is more than the minimum cash value that's required by your insurance company to maintain the policy.

What happens if the insurance company makes a redetermination and says I have to make higher premium payments?

You have a couple of options: (1) Pay the higher premiums and keep the same death benefits; (2) pay the lower premiums and receive lower death benefits.

What happens if I get lucky and find myself paying less for my interest-sensitive policy?

You can pay the lower premiums and keep the same death benefits, or you can keep paying the higher premiums and keep the same coverage. You can have the difference between the old and new premiums invested in your cash value. Or you may be able to use the difference in premiums to increase your death benefits. You will, however, have to qualify for more insurance coverage based on your health.

LIFE INSURANCE AS A SOURCE OF LOW-COST LOANS

Financial advisors often advise cash-strapped families to take out a low-cost loan from their life insurance.

Policyholders can borrow against 75 to 90 percent of the cash value that's built up in a life insurance policy. The cash value is the investment (or savings) portion of the policy.

Many people forget they can borrow from their life insurance. Gary Reidlinger, CPA/PFS, Bay City, MI, says, "Borrowing from existing policies can be beneficial because the rates are traditionally lower than the going market. Rates on insurance loans now range from 6 to 8 percent. You pay about 15 to 20 percent for unsecured personal loans and prime plus 2 percent or more for secured loans."

In addition to lower borrowing rates, life insurance loans have two other attractive features that can't be matched by other lending institutions. First, the loan doesn't have to be repaid within a set period of time—or ever. Policyholders can choose to let the interest accrue as new debt. The downside of choosing to do so is a decrease in the face value of the policy. For example, if an $8,000 loan on a $100,000 policy with $10,000 of cash value was not repaid, the beneficiary would receive $92,000 when the insured person dies.

The interest on the loan can be paid or rolled over as new debt that is tacked on to the existing policy loan.

The second feature is the ease with which a loan can be obtained. Unlike banks or finance companies that must do a credit check before making a secured or personal loan, life insurance companies are required to loan cash values automatically. As a result, many insurance companies will process a loan within three to five days upon verbal notification. Other firms require that a policy loan request form be filled out. After the insurance company receives the written request, it takes about a week to get the money.

The loan proceeds are not considered taxable income; otherwise a loan is a loan. In addition, the IRS has a strict set of rules on how much you must pay in premiums over a 7-year period. If you violate what is called the "7-pay test," you could end up paying income taxes on withdrawals or policy loans. (See Chapters 5 and 8 for IRS rules on UL premium payment rules.) If you let your policy lapse, you could have a taxable gain, which is the loan value in excess of the premiums you paid into the policy.

Despite the ease and flexibility of getting a life insurance loan, some experts stress that there are several negatives. For example, loans on whole life policies taken out in or after 1983 charge lending rates that vary annually based on the Moody's Corporate Bond Index. A policyholder might have to pay 10 percent interest on the loan. That's about 2 percent more than they are earning on the cash value in a fixed rate whole life policy. As a result, financial advisors encourage individuals to borrow from older policies they may own because the loan rates are lower. Pre-1980 policies typically charge 5 or 6 percent interest and mid-1980 policies charge 8 percent.

In addition, policyholders who borrow from variable rate or interest-sensitive policies sacrifice potential growth on their investments. Since your cash value fluctuates due to changes in the financial markets, insurance companies transfer cash values in stock and bond funds to accounts paying fixed rates that are 1 to 2 percent less than the loan rate. That protects the collateral in the event, for example, of a stock or bond market decline.

People can also get shortchanged when they borrow from a dividend-paying whole life policy (dividends are excess earnings that are paid to mutual life insurance policyholders). An appealing 8 percent loan could translate into an 11 percent loan. The reason: If the mutual insurance company's cost of borrowing the money is 11 percent, dividend payments may be cut by 3 percent to compensate for the shortfall in the cost of funds.

SHOULD YOU BUY TERM INSURANCE AND INVEST THE DIFFERENCE?

This is an age-old life insurance debate. Why pay all those fat commissions (over 50% in the first year) for cash value insurance when you can buy term insurance and invest the difference in a tax-free retirement savings account?

Those in Favor Say Yea

Those in favor recommend buying a cheap, annually renewable term policy and starting a savings plan on your own. That sounds like a better deal than giving all that money to a life insurance company when you buy a whole life policy.

Those in favor of buying term insurance also say that you are buying life insurance to provide income for your family in the event you die unexpectedly. The insurance will make up for the lost income during the years you would have been employed.

But what if you live to a ripe old age? What if you are about to retire at age 65 and want to move to Arizona or Florida? You are now thinking about living on a fixed income from your Social Security, your company pension plan, and your personal savings.

You could live another 15 years based on your life expectancy. So you have to make your money last. But now you find yourself spending your retirement income to keep your whole life policy in force.

To avoid this predicament, you should buy temporary protection until you retire. If you buy term and every year invest the savings from foregoing a whole life policy, you have an insurance policy and a savings account.

Say you bought a $100,000 term policy and can afford to invest $2,000 a year into an individual retirement account (IRA) that earns 7 percent tax free for 20 years—you take distributions when you retire. You will have amassed an extra kitty of about $88,000 to live on. Because of the high fees and commissions deducted from your premium payments, that could be a lot more money than you would get from a cash value policy that paid the same rate.

A word to the wise, however, about investing the difference in an IRA: A loan payout from a whole life policy for retirement income may outlast your IRA's bundle of cash. In addition, loans from a life insurance policy are not taxed, but you do pay taxes on your IRA distributions.

You have that extra $88,000, plus your pension, Social Security, and your other assets to live on. All your assets add up to more than the face value of the insurance you purchased in the first place. Besides, most of the death benefit proceeds in your whole life policy after 20 years are cash value.

So why bother buying whole life insurance? If you invested the $2,000 a year with the insurance company, they take out big 1st- and 2nd-year commissions. Just check to see what the surrender value of your policy equals after the first two policy years. You also have to pay mortality fees and administrative charges. After all the costs are deducted, that 7 percent illustration your cash value policy pays you could be reduced to around a 5.9 percent internal rate of return.

Why pay the insurance company all that money when you can buy term and invest the difference in no-load mutual funds that have no sales charges? By diversifying in stocks, bonds, and money market funds, you can earn as much or more than the amount paid by your insurance company. If you invest in a no-load mutual fund IRA, your money will grow, and the tax will be deferred because it is in a retirement savings account.

A recent study by Peter Katt published in the *American Association for Individual Investors Journal* in 1990 showed how buying term insurance and investing the difference can be a better deal than investing in a full commission cash value policy. The commissions and charges eat away at the value of the investments, especially during the earlier years.

Katt compared a full commission 5-year level term policy (renewable every five years) with a full commission universal life insurance policy. He assumed a 38-year-old nonsmoker bought $600,000 of coverage. In addition, the universal policy paid 8.5 percent annual interest over 8 years. He also assumed that the difference in premium payments between the term and universal policy were invested in a side fund that earned 5.95 percent after taxes.

By the time our 38-year-old male was about to turn 58, he had $75,299 in his side fund. That was substantially more than the cash value in the universal policy. At the same age, there was $68,327 in the cash value policy.

Those Opposed Say Nay

The naysayers disagree. Contrary to popular belief, buying term insurance and investing the difference instead of taking out a whole life policy is difficult to do. It can also be risky.

William Brownlie, author of *The Life Insurance Buyer's Guide* (New York: McGraw Hill, 1989), says it's a myth that you save on sales commissions by buying term insurance compared with whole life, if you intend to keep the policy for a long time. He adds that you may take too much risk on the investment portion of a "buy term and invest the difference" tactic, compared with getting a whole life policy. However, just buying term insurance based on your financial condition may be an affordable way to obtain some protection.

"When you are considering buying term insurance and investing the difference, the sole consideration is: What would you have to earn in compound interest in a self-determined investment vehicle to have exactly the same income tax-exempt death benefit as would be provided by a nonterm policy?" says Brownlie, a CLU and ChFC from Chelmsford, MA.

He adds, however, that you must have the discipline to invest every year. So, in some years you would have to earn high rates to match the whole life policy.

Assuming a 45-year-old nonsmoker took out a $100,000 policy, Brownlie says the break-even point on some current term versus whole life policies is based on the following:

- You have to spend exactly the same amount of money for whole life as you spend for term insurance and an outside investment: $2,001 was used each year from age 45 to 65.
- Every year an amount of term is to be purchased which, when combined with the separate investment, must equal exactly the following: the same amount of money or cash

Wealth Building Worksheet

Comparing Whole Life Policies

	Policy A	*Policy B*	*Policy C*
Amount of insurance	$____	$____	$____
Annual premium	$____	$____	$____
Guaranteed cash value rate (%)	____	____	____
Guaranteed cash value growth			
5 years	$____	$____	$____
10 years	____	____	____
15 years	____	____	____
20 years	____	____	____
Accumulated value of the dividends			
5 years	$____	$____	$____
10 years	____	____	____
15 years	____	____	____
20 years	____	____	____
Amount of insurance via paid up additions			
5 years	$____	$____	$____
10 years	____	____	____
15 years	____	____	____
20 years	____	____	____
Cash surrender value			
5 years	$____	$____	$____
10 years	____	____	____
15 years	____	____	____
20 years	____	____	____
Internal rate of return on surrender (%)			
5 years	____	____	____
10 years	____	____	____
15 years	____	____	____
20 years	____	____	____
Interest-adjusted cost index			
5 years	$____	____	____
10 years	____	____	____
15 years	____	____	____
20 years	____	____	____

Wealth Building Worksheet *(Cont'd)*

	Policy A	*Policy B*	*Policy C*
What's the loan rate?	$_____	$_____	$_____
Is there direct recognition?	_____	_____	_____
Financial strength ratings			
A.M. Best	_____	_____	_____
Standard & Poor's	_____	_____	_____
Moody's	_____	_____	_____
Duff & Phelps	_____	_____	_____

surrender value and exactly the same tax-exempt death benefit provided by the whole life policy; or exactly the same amount of paid-up life insurance with its increasing reserve and the yearly paid-up dividends received by the owner of the whole life policy as a living capital formation benefit.

His analysis reveals that if you don't need insurance beyond 10 years, term is better. But the longer the holding period, the higher the annual rate you have to make on an investment coupled with term insurance. For 15 years, you would have to earn 8.19 percent annually to have the same amount as a whole life policy with a cash surrender value of $43,890 and a total tax-exempt death benefit of $135,297. For 20 years, a 9.44 percent annual return would give you the same as a whole life policy that had a $79,762 cash surrender value and a $180,071 tax-exempt death benefit.

POINTS TO REMEMBER

- Whole life insurance provides protection for your entire lifetime.
- The premiums remain the same until you cash out your policy or claims are paid to your beneficiaries.

- The death benefits (the face amount of the policy) stay the same for the life of the policy.
- You can borrow against the cash value of your policy at relatively low rates. If you don't pay back the loan, however, the death benefits are reduced by the amount of the loan plus the amount of the accumulated interest.
- You can buy whole life-type insurance that pays a fixed rate on the cash value. You can also buy whole life that pays variable rates based on market conditions.
- You can use the dividends that mutual insurance companies pay to policyholders at the end of the year in different ways: to buy more insurance, reinvest in your cash value, or to pay part of your premiums.
- Insurance policies that use your dividends to pay off the policy early are called vanishing premium policies.
- Most people buy whole life insurance because they get insurance plus a tax-free savings component.
- If you are concerned about the impact of inflation on your death benefits, you can get a cost-of-living rider on your policy. That way your coverage will keep pace with inflation. You can also get a living benefit rider. This enables you to use some of your death benefits early to pay hospital bills when you are seriously ill.
- You and your spouse can joint-insure. When you buy a first-to-die policy, the insurance pays death benefits when the first spouse dies. The surviving spouse will get the proceeds and possibly still have insurance coverage. You can also buy a second-to-die policy. People with large estates buy policies that pay off when the second spouse passes on. The proceeds are often used to pay estate taxes.

8

Universal Life Insurance

THE FLEXIBLE WAY TO BUY

Universal life (UL) policies are cash value policies that have more options than whole life insurance. With most whole life insurance, people pay the same premiums every year and their death benefits stay the same. ULs have more bells and whistles than whole life policies.

First, you earn market rates of interest on your cash value, not fixed rates as with a whole life policy. Consider these total return ranges:

- Intermediate-term corporate bond returns could range from 3.6 to 6.2 percent.
- Long-term U.S. government bond returns could range from 1.3 to 8 percent.
- Three-month Treasury bill returns could range from 1.6 to 5 percent.

Second, your premiums and death benefits can vary along with your financial condition. Third, if you want to invest in stock and bond mutual funds rather than be paid by your insurance company, you can buy a universal variable policy (UVL). Chapter 9 covers this option in more detail.

Benson Coulter, CPA, CFP, and president of First Financial Planners, Inc., North Palm Beach, FL, contends that many people buy UL policies because of their flexibility. "Young couples buy a policy, and later cut back their premiums after they purchase a home. . . . [L]ater on they will increase their premiums [because] they need more protection and tax-deferred buildup on their cash value. Universal life also pays competitive rates. . . ."

TWO FLAVORS OF UNIVERSAL LIFE

You have two options when you buy a universal policy.

Option A

Premium payments can decrease or increase within allowable limits, but the death benefit coverage remains the same.

If you use option A, your cash value and your death benefits add up to give you a level amount of death benefits. If you have a $100,000 policy that has accumulated $50,000 in cash value, your beneficiaries would collect a death benefit that's half a return of their cash value and half pure insurance.

But suppose you don't die, and you keep on paying your premiums. At age 95, the cash value in the policy will equal the death benefits. Before that time, there must be a gap between the cash value and the death benefits. In certain circumstances, your death benefits can increase above the face amount of the policy. This occurs if the cash values grow more quickly than expected due to high interest rates. An adjustment must be made based on IRS rules.

Option A policies may have one exception under which death benefits can increase. As long as you have enough cash value to pay for the cost, you can buy additional insurance. However, if you try to boost your level of death benefits too high, the insurance company may ask you to take a medical exam to prove that you are in good health and can qualify for the extra coverage.

Option B

Your death benefits increase or decrease with the growth of your cash value.

If you pay higher premiums and the cash value grows at a high rate of interest, your death benefits will increase. Conversely, if your cash value earns less money or you reduce your premium payments, the death benefits will decrease. The death benefits cannot go lower than the face amount of the policy.

How do I decide between option A and option B?

If higher cash value is your goal, then option A is the answer. Option B is better if you want your insurance coverage to increase over the years.

WEALTH BUILDING PROFILE ***A Flexible Premium Policy.*** Jim, age 35, is a nonsmoker who purchased a $200,000 UL policy. He is married and has one child. He picked option B because he liked the idea of the increasing death benefits. As his wages increase and lifestyle improves, so will his family's protection. In addition, he still has the flexibility to adjust his premium payments as necessary.

Jim's financial planner set him up with a level premium of $1,332 a year. Assuming the interest credited to the cash value grows at 8.3 percent a year, the cash value in the account accumulates to $13,552 and $45,849 after 10 and 20 years respectively. His death benefits will grow to $215,322 after 10 years and to $245,849 after 20 years.

By the time Jim reaches age 70, the policy is paid up and the death benefits equal $346,614.

You get a guaranteed level of death benefits and a guaranteed rate of 4 to 4.5 percent credited to your cash value. These protect you in case interest rates drop to abysmal levels.

There are limits on how much you can increase your insurance coverage under option B. You get automatic increases as your cash value grows. You can also get a cost-of-living rider attached to your policy so that your death benefits increase with inflation. Again, however, if you increase your premium payments and your death benefits too much based on the insurance company's guidelines, you may have to get a medical exam to provide evidence of insurability.

A LIFE CYCLE INSURANCE POLICY

Whether you use option A or B, UL is the kind of insurance that can change when your lifestyle and financial needs and goals change.

Figure 8–1 provides an example of UL flexibility. Refer to the letters on the figure that match the text.

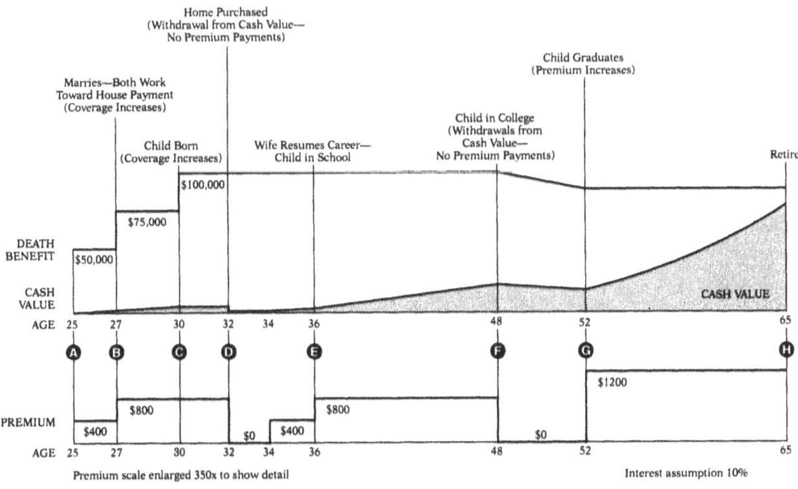

(Source: *Universal Life Basics.* Indianapolis, IN: Pictorial, Inc.)

Figure 8–1
Universal Life Insurance

A. A 25-year-old nonsmoking male buys a $50,000 UL policy for an annual premium of $400.

B. Two years later, he marries. The couple puts $800 into the policy and boosts the death benefits to $75,000.

C. Three years later, when the husband is age 30, their child is born. So the family increases their coverage to $100,000 without having to increase their premium payments.

D. Two years later, the family buys a new home. So they borrow $4,000 from their policy to help with the down payment. They also stop paying premiums for a couple of years.

E. When the husband is age 34, they resume paying $400 premiums. Two years later, their child enters school, and the wife goes back to work. So the family boosts their premiums back up to $800. They want to save some extra money for their child's college education.

F. The child enters college. The family stops paying premiums and withdraws $2,500 a year from the cash value to help pay educational expenses. The death benefits drop because of their withdrawals.

G. The child graduates from college four years later. Now the couple boosts their premiums to $1,200 a year. They want to save extra money for their retirement.

H. When the husband is age 65, the couple stops paying premiums. They withdraw cash as an added source of retirement income.

ACTION ITEM

Don't worry about falling interest rates when you own a UL policy. The insurance company will guarantee they will pay you at least 4 to 4.5 percent interest on your cash value.

ACTION ITEM

Be careful about cutting back too far on your UL premiums. There are limits on how much you can reduce or increase your premium payments. If you don't pay enough, you may get a notice from your insurer saying you have 30 to 60 days to make the extra payments.

Can I put as much as I want into my UL policy every year?

The tax laws place limits on UL contributions. As discussed earlier, you have to be careful about putting too much money into your policy in relation to your death benefits. Your insurance agent will show you the minimum and maximum amounts you can put in every year before you violate the tax rules. If you do not adhere to these rules, you could find yourself paying taxes when you withdraw, borrow money, or surrender your policy.

WHAT YOU SEE IS WHAT YOU GET WHEN YOU PURCHASE UNIVERSAL

Life insurance textbooks say that UL is transparent. That means, when you look at an illustration, you see exactly what you pay, how much the insurance company charges you in fees, and what your cash value and death benefits grow to. In addition, the annual report you receive on your policy will also show each component of your policy, as well as the current interest rate paid.

It works this way: After you make your premium payment, the insurance company takes out money for expenses and a mortality fee. Then they pay you interest on the remaining money. That principal and interest equal your cash value. In the next year, the insurance company adds your cash value to your premium payment, subtracts expenses and mortality fees, then adds in interest income to get your new year-end cash value.

The mortality fees are higher if you use option B because the death benefits increase as your policy matures. Over the long term, insurance companies know they will pay out more dollars for death benefits, so they have to charge you higher mortality fees to cover the cost.

THERE ARE DRAWBACKS

Despite the many advantages of a UL, there are some drawbacks: (1) The insurance company can raise its mortality fees in the future; (2) if interest rates stay low for a sustained period, the cash values will not grow as fast as you anticipated; (3) if you don't faithfully contribute to your UL, you will defeat the purpose of buying cash value life insurance—income protection for the family.

Watch Those Loads

Some policies have front-end loads or commissions. Others charge a back-end load when you surrender the policy. And some policies have both front- and back-end loads.

Most newer policies have back-end surrender costs, but few companies charge something at both ends. Front-end loads usually range from 7 to 10 percent.

Hidden Fees

Some insurance companies don't pay you the extra interest over the guaranteed rate on the first $1,000 of your cash value. For example, if you are earning 8.5 percent on your cash value, $85 should be credited to your cash value on that thousand dollars. Instead, the insurance company only credits the 4.5

percent—or $45—stipulated in your policy. The insurance company is essentially charging you a load of $40 on your first $1,000 of cash value.

To get an idea of what you are paying in loads, ask for the internal rate of return (IRR) on your policy. The difference between the IRR and the interest credited to your policy represents fees and charges.

ACTION ITEM

Check the internal rate of return on your cash surrender value. That way you know what you make after the insurance company deducts its fees and expenses. Say your UL illustration shows you the insurance company is paying you 9 percent interest on your policy. If you surrender the policy after 10 years, the cash surrender value is $14,372. You really earned 6.5 percent annually, assuming you made $1,000 premium payments every year.

Load fees are not the only way an insurance company can make back its expenses and profit margins. There may be an annual expense charge, an annual fee, or a high policy fee. Alternatively, the insurance company may take its piece of the profits before they credit your account or increase the mortality charges to the maximum allowable rate.

Some policies charge "excess interest" when the policy is surrendered. You only get credit with the guaranteed rate of interest for the last year of your policy. It works the same way as the hidden front-end charges described earlier, but the extra earnings are deducted in the final year of the policy.

Watch Those Loans, Too

Remember what direct recognition means? If you borrow $10,000 against your cash value, the insurance company takes

$10,000 from your cash value and invests the money at 2 percent less than your loan rate. The remainder of your cash value earns current rates. So if you had $25,000 in cash value and you borrowed $10,000, only $15,000 would earn current rates.

Federal Taxes

The IRS puts limits on how much you can put into a universal policy. In the past, some people dumped a great deal of money into the policy at once. They used the insurance as a tax shelter because the cash value isn't taxed. Then they borrowed money out of the policy at below-market rates.

WEALTH BUILDING PROFILE

Maximum Premium Limits. Jack, age 43, is a nonsmoker. He bought $100,000 of UL coverage. His agent suggested that he make annual premium payments of at least $800 for the sake of discipline.

Under tax guidelines, the maximum single amount he could pay into this policy is $19,886. The maximum annual amount he can put in is $1,665 over 20 years. And the maximum he could pay annually for 7 years is $4,431.

If Jack violates these rules, the policy will be considered an MEC. As a result, if he borrows against the cash value in the policy, withdraws money, or surrenders the policy, he will first pay taxes on the gain in the policy. The gain is the amount of money you have when you subtract the total amount of premiums paid from the cash value of the policy. So, for example, if Jack borrowed $10,000 from his policy, violated the premiums payment rules, and had a gain of $3,000, he would pay a fine of 10 percent on the gain plus income tax since he is under age 59½. Assuming Jack was in the 28 percent tax bracket, he would owe the IRS a total of $870 on April 15.

The IRS places strict limits on how much can be paid into a universal policy over a given time period. If too much is paid into the policy under the 7-pay test, the insurance policy is considered a modified endowment contract (MEC).

The IRS has a complicated formula that says premiums can't exceed certain levels over a 7-year period. And if a policyholder makes a lump-sum payment, it can't exceed certain limits, as shown in the following profile.

Stick to the required premium payment schedule. If you think you will need more insurance coverage in the future, you should consider getting a cost-of-living rider on your policy. That way you won't have to worry about overcontributing to your policy.

Your Earnings Are Uncertain

Interest rates can bounce around, but fortunately, you don't have to worry about losing money or earning a measly 2 percent if interest rates plunge because insurance companies guarantee you will get a rate of 4 to 4.5 percent.

Check Your Net Earnings

After commissions, expenses, mortality fees, and any load charges are subtracted from your policy values, you earn less than the credit rate of interest. That's because charges are deducted from the cash value before your account is credited with interest earnings. The internal rate of return (IRR) is the true rate of interest earned on the cash value of your policy. The IRR tells you what you really earn if you make *X* amount of annual premium payments.

Table 8–1 shows what you would earn on a $100,000 UL policy into which you put $1,000 per year, assuming the insurance company does not pay dividends.

ACTION ITEM

Some firms use the new rate method to credit interest on cash value. That method is based on what the company earns on new money it receives from policyholders' premiums. This method works best when interest rates are rising. Other companies use the portfolio method to calculate interest. This method bases payouts on what the insurance company's total investment assets are earning on both old and new money. This method pays more when interest rates are falling because the insurance company is locking into investments that mature over a longer time.

Table 8–1
How Your $1,000 Annual Premiums Grow

What You Earn	*Grows to $*	
(IRR %)	*Over 10 Years*	*Over 20 Years*
5.0	$13,207	$34,719
5.5	13,583	36,786
6.0	13,972	38,993
6.5	14,372	41,349
7.0	14,784	43,865
7.5	15.208	46,553
8.0	15,645	49,423
8.5	16,096	52,489
9.0	16,560	55,765
9.5	17,039	55,765
10.0	17,531	63,002

TAX-FREE PENSION MONEY

In addition to buying income protection for your family, you can use UL as a tax-deferred savings for your golden years because life insurance loans are not taxed. So you can borrow against the cash value in your policy every year as a source of tax-free income.

Here's how you could set up a universal life insurance policy to give you tax-free retirement income:

A male, age 40, who was a nonsmoker would make premium payments of $5,000 a year for 19 years and receive $500,000 of death benefit coverage. Assuming the cash value grew at a 7.5 percent internal rate of return—that's the return made after fees, commissions, and other charges have been deducted from the policy—the money would grow to $220,715 by the time the 40-year-old was 60 years of age.

At age 60, the policyholder could borrow $16,024 a year against the cash value over the next 35 years. At age 95, there would not be much in the way of death benefits. Death benefits are reduced by the policy loans and accumulated loan interests. But at age 80, the policyholder would still have $215,000 in death benefits.

Although universal life insurance can be a source of tax-free income during retirement, there are the following drawbacks:

1. The insurance industry is on shaky ground due to junk bond and real estate investment losses. To protect against this, consumers should only do business with insurance companies that carry top ratings from firms such as A.M. Best, Standard & Poor's, Moody's, and Duff and Phelps.
2. There's no guarantee the interest rate in the life insurance illustration will be used to calculate your cash value over the years. If interest rates stay low over the next 10 years, a 7 percent rate of return could be an overestimated rate. Most insurance companies guarantee they will pay you 4.5 percent. If you earn that rate, you won't be getting those fat retirement checks.

3. If your payment schedule violates the tax laws, your loans might be considered taxable income. You would have to pay income tax on the amount that is in excess of the premiums paid into the policy.

Wealth Building Worksheet

Comparing Universal Life Policies

	Policy A	*Policy B*	*Policy C*
Amount of insurance	$_____	$_____	$_____
Premium schedule	$_____	$_____	$_____
Guaranteed rate (%)	_____	_____	_____
Current rate (%)	_____	_____	_____
Cash value growth on level premiums at guaranteed rate			
5 years	$_____	$_____	$_____
10 years	_____	_____	_____
15 years	_____	_____	_____
20 years	_____	_____	_____
At 8% interest			
5 years	$_____	$_____	$_____
10 years	_____	_____	_____
15 years	_____	_____	_____
20 years	_____	_____	_____
At 10% interest			
5 years	$_____	$_____	$_____
10 years	_____	_____	_____
15 years	_____	_____	_____
20 years	_____	_____	_____
Cash surrender value at guaranteed rate			
5 years	$_____	$_____	$_____
10 years	_____	_____	_____
15 years	_____	_____	_____
20 years	_____	_____	_____
At 8% interest			
5 years	$_____	$_____	$_____
10 years	_____	_____	_____
15 years	_____	_____	_____
20 years	_____	_____	_____

Wealth Building Worksheet *(Cont'd)*

	Policy A	*Policy B*	*Policy C*
At 10% interest			
5 years	$_____	$_____	$_____
10 years	_____	_____	_____
15 years	_____	_____	_____
20 years	_____	_____	_____
Policy loan rate (%)	_____	_____	_____
Interest-adjusted cost index			
10 years	$_____	$_____	$_____
20 years	_____	_____	_____
Financial strength ratings			
A.M. Best	_____	_____	_____
Standard & Poor's	_____	_____	_____
Moody's	_____	_____	_____
Duff & Phelps	_____	_____	_____

POINTS TO REMEMBER

- UL is a flexible premium policy, so you don't have to pay the same premiums for life insurance coverage every year.
- You earn current rates of interest on your cash value with a UL policy. The rates can change from year to year, but most insurance companies guarantee they will pay at least 4 to 4.5 percent on the policy's cash value.
- Some UL policies are considered variable universal policies. You can make flexible premium payments and invest in common stock and bond mutual funds (see Chapter 9).
- You can pick between two types of UL coverage. Your death benefits stay the same if you purchase option A. Under option B of a UL policy, your death benefits would grow in line with your cash value.
- Before you purchase a UL policy, be sure to check the surrender and interest-adjusted cost index and review the illustration carefully.

9

Variable Life Insurance

Variable life insurance may be right for you if you are a do-it-yourself type person, comfortable investing in common stock and bond mutual funds, willing to accept short-term losses for long-term gains, and have the time to manage investments. That's because the essence of a variable life insurance policy is that part of your premium payments buys term insurance and part is invested in bonds, money market funds, and common stock mutual funds both here and overseas. Meanwhile, your money is protected against an insurance company default because the investment portion of your payment goes into a separate account at a custodian bank that also acts as the trustee. Creditors of an insurance company cannot lay claim to your money. The account is under your name—just as if it were a passbook savings account.

→ ACTION ITEM ←

Whether you buy a variable or whole life policy, the investment earnings are not taxed because they are part of an insurance policy. However, the IRS places limits on the amount

you can pay into your policy without paying income tax on withdrawals or loans from your policy.

Ben Baldwin, CLU, CFP, and ChFC, president of Baldwin Financial Systems, Northbrook, IL, favors the universal version of variable life insurance, which is discussed here, over whole life and term life insurance, because of the investment choices. The buildup of cash values can be tremendous during strong periods in the stock market. Over the past 10 years, for example, experts say that the average stock market mutual fund has doubled in value.

As a result, according to Baldwin, profits can be taken out of stocks and locked up in a fixed rate account with annual investment options offered by many variable life insurance policies. The rapid accumulation of funds enables policyholders to have an extra source of retirement income or to pay for a child's college education. Policyholders can also take advantage of the current tax laws and borrow against the cash value of their policy without having to worry about paying taxes on the money. If they owned an annuity or retirement savings account and took money out before that age, they would pay a 10 percent fine and ordinary income tax on the withdrawal.

HOW VARIABLE LIFE INSURANCE WORKS

There are two types of variable life insurance. With the first type, you make single or level premium payments and invest the cash value in a choice of mutual funds. With the second type, you manage the cash value in your policy the way you see fit. This option, which is known as "universal variable life," gives you payments as your financial condition changes.

ACTION ITEM

Many fees are attached to variable life insurance policies. Whichever option you choose, you may be hit with a load fee or commission, a mortality fee, a management fee of ½ to 1 percent, and other expenses.

ACTION ITEM

When you buy variable life insurance, do business with financial planners or agents who are called *registered representatives.* Registered representatives are licensed to sell securities and are regulated by the National Association of Securities Dealers.

Death Benefits

The death benefits of the variable policy are tied to the returns on the cash value. However, your premium provides your beneficiaries with a guaranteed minimum amount of death benefits no matter how your mutual funds perform.

If your investment outperforms the insurance company's assumed rate of return (usually 4 percent or 4.5 percent), the insurance company takes the difference in the values or the excess interest and buys you more life insurance coverage. Conversely, if your investments underperform the assumed rate of return, the insurance company may not buy you extra insurance coverage.

You Get the Same Riders and Options as Whole Life

You can buy variable life insurance from participating or nonparticipating companies. Participating companies distribute dividends, nonparticipating companies do not.

You can get the same riders and options with variable life as you can get with whole life, too. Here's a list:

- Waiver of premium.
- Accidental death benefits.
- Term insurance on other family members.
- Cost-of-living increase in coverage.
- Survivor options (insurance pays death benefit when the surviving spouse dies).

Special Provisions When You Borrow Money

You can take tax-free loans against the cash value in the policy. Loan rates run about 8 to 10 percent. Your cash value serves as collateral for the loan. Here's how it works: The insurance company takes the money out of your mutual funds and puts the proceeds in a fixed rate account that earns about 2 percent less than your loan interest. That way the company doesn't face the risk of seeing its collateral drop in value if the stock or bond markets decline.

What Do You Want to Invest In?

You have numerous investment options when you own a variable life insurance policy. Chapter 11 discusses how to invest your cash values to get the best returns for the least amount of risk. For now, let's look at the advantages and investment options of mutual funds.

There are several advantages to investing in variable life compared with whole life or other types of interest-sensitive cash value policies.

- Most insurance companies offer you a choice of mutual funds. You can switch among a stable of mutual funds as investment conditions or your financial needs change. When interest rates are high, you can invest in mutual funds that invest in money market accounts. When rates come down and stocks perform well, you can switch into funds that buy equities. Or you can switch investments among stocks, bonds, and cash. That way you hedge your bets and protect your portfolio in the event of a stock market plunge.

- You get diversification. Mutual funds pool investors' money and buy securities. The funds hold a large number of shares of stocks or bonds, so that the entire portfolio won't lose too much money if a few issues perform poorly.
- You get professional management. Your investment is being managed by a professional called a *portfolio manager.* The manager has a staff of analysts who evaluate securities as well as economic conditions. The fund managers evaluate the information they get from their analysts and make the investment decisions. A fund manager, for example, may change the investment mix of the mutual fund to take advantage of anticipated changes in the economy. For example, when the economy is coming out of a recession and interest rates start to drop, small company stocks may outperform the market averages. When rates come down, interest-rate-sensitive utility stocks do well. When inflation heats up, natural resource stocks do well.

Keep in mind that mutual fund managers try to buy stock in companies that have high expected earnings and cheap stock prices. In other words, they want to buy stock in companies they perceive as undervalued.

Bond fund managers lengthen or shorten the average maturities of their portfolios in anticipation of changes in interest rates. Bond prices and interest rates move in opposite directions: When interest rates rise, bond prices fall; conversely, when interest rates fall, bond prices rise.

Since the longer maturity bonds show greater changes in price to a given change in interest rates, some fund managers will adjust the average maturity of the fund. If rates are expected to rise, they keep money in short-term maturities or cash investments such as T-bills, large-denomination bank CDs, and commercial paper (corporate IOUs). That way, they reinvest maturing securities at higher rates without seeing the market value of the bonds decline. When rates seem to be dropping, fund managers will invest longer term. They lock into higher rates. In addition, the market value of the bonds goes up as rates come down.

NOT ALL MUTUAL FUNDS ARE ALIKE

Mutual funds have different investment objectives. Some funds invest for growth and profits, others invest for income and safety.

Some mutual funds have the potential to earn 30 percent or more in a year. They can also lose 20 percent or more in a year. That's called the risk versus return trade-off of investing. The bigger the risk or the greater the chance of losing money, the bigger the potential return. The lower the risk, the lower—but safer—the return.

Over the short term, you can lose more money in riskier mutual funds that, for example, invest in over-the-counter small company stocks compared with funds that buy blue chip stocks or Treasury bonds. Over the long term, however, you can make the risk work for you and build your wealth.

For example, financial research published by the American Association for Individual Investors shows that the longer you hold stocks, the less chance you have of losing money. Over the past six decades, the results showed the following:

- If you bought and held blue chip stocks for one year, you would have lost money 30 percent of the time. But blue chip stocks have averaged a 10 percent return over the past 60 years.
- You would have lost money 32 percent of the time if you owned small company stocks. These stocks, however, have racked up 12 percent annually in returns over the same time period.
- If you owned T-bills, you never lost a penny. But these risk-free investments have averaged just 4 percent a year over the past 60 years.

Table 9–1 shows the low- and high-risk investment choices offered by variable life insurance policies. The lowest risk investments are money funds. Money funds keep their net asset value of $1. They keep the maturity less than 150 days and invest in Treasury bills and the most creditworthy banks and corporations.

Government bond funds that invest in Treasury securities and government agency bonds are lower risk than corporate bonds. The investments are backed directly or indirectly against default by the U.S. government. But the bond prices change as interest rates change. So if interest rates rose, you could lose money if you had to sell your individual bonds or bond fund shares.

Next in line are corporate bond and income funds. These funds are low- to moderate-risk investments. Income funds invest in high-dividend-paying common and preferred stock and high-quality corporate bonds. High-grade corporate bond funds invest in the most creditworthy issues rated BBB or better by Standard & Poor's and Moody's.

You encounter moderate risks when you invest in common stocks. Blue chip stocks, the lowest risk common stocks, are issued by large and well-established corporations such as

Table 9–1
Investment Pyramid

High Risk
- Junk bond funds
- Sector funds
- Aggressive growth funds
- Growth funds
- Growth and income funds
- Income funds and corporate bond funds
- Government bond funds
- Short-term bond funds
- Money market funds

Low Risk
- Government securities money funds

Exxon and AT&T. Growth and income funds primarily invest in blue chip stocks.

Higher risk mutual funds invest in growth stock companies. These smaller firms can show tremendous earnings growth rates. There is always a risk, however, that the company could fall on hard times. Since growth stocks don't pay dividends, investors have no income source to cushion losses when the stock's price drops.

In addition to growth stocks, precious metals mining company stock, overseas stocks, and junk bonds or poor credit rating bond issuers are also high-risk investments.

WEALTH BUILDING PROFILE ***Growth from Common Stock Mutual Funds.*** Judy, age 34, feels comfortable investing in stocks. So she purchased a $100,000 variable life insurance policy because she could invest in common stock mutual funds. She also chose the level premium variable life policy over the flexible premium policy. She favors paying the same amount of premiums every year for a couple of reasons. First, she likes the discipline of being required to pay a fixed amount every year. In addition, she dislikes the idea of having to pay in extra premiums if her investments in a universal policy perform poorly.

Her financial planner showed her how stocks have historically grown at a 10 percent annual rate. And Judy believes that, over the long term, a well-managed mutual fund will outperform fixed rate accounts. As a result, she will have some extra cash value over the planner's projection. She can use the money for retirement. Since the death benefits will increase as the cash value grows, her loved ones will also have an extra layer of protection in the event of her unexpected death.

Assuming her premium payments are $1,570 a year, she will have a cash surrender value of $15,799 and death benefits of $107,519 after 10 years if the investment grows at an annual rate of 8 percent. By the time she's age 65 in the 30th policy year, the cash surrender value is $94,741 and she'll have death benefits of $173,150, at 8 percent.

No one knows for sure how the stock market will perform over the next 30 years. But even if her investments perform poorly, she knows her beneficiaries will get $100,000. The insurance company guarantees $100,000 of coverage.

WEALTH BUILDING PROFILE ***Extra Insurance Coverage.*** Grant, age 60, bought a variable universal policy 10 years ago. He needed some additional coverage on the family. He also liked the idea of investing in the stock market without having to pay taxes on the dividend and capital gains reinvested in the mutual fund.

Grant plans to pay planned annual premiums of $3,740 for $200,000 of coverage. His death benefits equal the face amount of the policy plus an extra amount of coverage if the investments have performed above the guaranteed rate on the contract.

At age 50, he was planning for the future. He wanted an extra source of retirement income in addition to his company pension. He also wanted to be sure his wife and children had enough income protection. He already had $250,000 of coverage from a whole life policy he had purchased 20 years ago. But his financial planner suggested he needed more coverage for the family and to cover a mortgage debt on a vacation home.

Today, he's enjoying the returns on his life insurance investments, his grandchildren, and his vacation home on the seashore.

He put two-thirds of his cash value in a growth stock mutual fund and one-third in a money fund as a hedge. Over the past 10 years, the investment has grown to $41,646 assuming he surrendered or cashed out his policy. His investment grew at a 9.45 percent annual rate of return. Less the insurance company's fees and charges, he earned 8.25 percent annually. The 8.25 percent translates into a taxable equivalent yield of

11 percent. That means he would have had to make 11 percent on a taxable investment to earn 8.25 percent after taxes since he is in the 28 percent federal tax bracket.

In addition, his death benefits now total $241,968. But when he retires at age 65, assuming his investment grows at the same rate, his cash surrender value will equal $72,531. His death benefits, at that time, will total $272,531.

I am interested in buying a variable life insurance policy. Should I buy the policy where I make the same premium payments every year or should I get the flexible premium variable policy?

You have to look at the advantages and disadvantages of both types of variable life insurance.

There are several pluses and minuses to level premium variable life insurance. On the plus side, you get life insurance protection and have a choice of diversified and professionally managed mutual funds to invest in. You can change your investment mix as economic conditions or your financial needs change. And the investments are not taxed by Uncle Sam.

Even if your common stock investments perform poorly, you won't have to pay higher premiums than you agreed to pay when you signed the life insurance contract. Not only that, you don't have to worry about the face amount decreasing below the original face amount due to declines in the value of your mutual fund investment. No matter how your investments perform, if you bought $200,000 in death benefits, it will not drop below that amount.

The disadvantages of the old style, level-premium policies, according to Baldwin, include high fees and expenses that reduce the return on your investments and lack of flexibility because you can't increase or decrease your premium payments or face amount of your policy as your financial needs change.

What are the pros and cons of the new universal variable life insurance policies?

If you are considering a universal variable policy, you also have to look at its advantages and disadvantages. On the plus side, you can adjust your premium payments. For example, Baldwin notes that his son invested heavily in his policy during his yuppy years. But he cut his universal variable premiums $100 a month after the birth of his first child. Later on, when his son bought a new home and had a second child, he cut the premium again.

In addition, conservative investors can keep part of their portfolio within a fixed rate account, which is one of the investment options in many variable policies. They can use the account as a parking place to salt away the profits from the other mutual fund investments.

You can also use the earnings in the guaranteed fixed rate account to pay for the cost of the insurance. You keep enough money in this investment vehicle to cover the expenses and mortality fees. This tactic allows you to pay for your term insurance with what is categorized as pretax earnings on the account. Then all other money is invested for long-term growth in mutual funds.

The big disadvantage of flexible variable life insurance is that the insurance company may ask you to make some extra premium payments if you have invested very little in your policy, the investment has performed poorly, and the expenses and mortality costs increase to the maximum allowable level that's stated in your contract.

Wealth Building Worksheet

Comparing Variable Life Policies

	Policy A	*Policy B*	*Policy C*
Amount of insurance	$_____	$_____	$_____
Premium schedule	$_____	$_____	$_____
Guaranteed rate (%)	_____	_____	_____
Current rate (%)	_____	_____	_____
Cash value growth on level premiums at guaranteed rate			
5 years	$_____	$_____	$_____
10 years	_____	_____	_____
15 years	_____	_____	_____
20 years	_____	_____	_____
At 8% interest			
5 years	$_____	$_____	$_____
10 years	_____	_____	_____
15 years	_____	_____	_____
20 years	_____	_____	_____
At 10% interest			
5 years	$_____	$_____	$_____
10 years	_____	_____	_____
15 years	_____	_____	_____
20 years	_____	_____	_____
Cash surrender value at guaranteed rate			
5 years	$_____	$_____	$_____
10 years	_____	_____	_____
15 years	_____	_____	_____
20 years	_____	_____	_____
At 8% interest			
5 years	$_____	$_____	$_____
10 years	_____	_____	_____
15 years	_____	_____	_____
20 years	_____	_____	_____
At 10% interest			
5 years	$_____	$_____	$_____
10 years	_____	_____	_____
15 years	_____	_____	_____
20 years	_____	_____	_____

Wealth Building Worksheet *(Cont'd)*

	Policy A	*Policy B*	*Policy C*
Policy loan rate (%)	_____	_____	_____
Interest-adjusted cost index			
10 years	$_____	$_____	$_____
20 years	_____	_____	_____
Financial strength ratings			
A.M. Best	_____	_____	_____
Standard & Poor's	_____	_____	_____
Moody's	_____	_____	_____
Duff & Phelps	_____	_____	_____

1. What premium will you pay for the amount of insurance you're buying?
2. What's the guaranteed cash value accumulation over 5, 10, 15, and 20 years?
3. What's the accumulated value of the dividends based on the insurance company's current history? How much do you accumulate over 5, 10, 15, and 20 years? How much insurance do the dividends buy if you have a policy with paid-up additions?
4. What's the cash surrender value of the policy after 5, 10, 15, and 20 years?
5. What's the internal rate of return on the cash surrender value?
6. What are the interest-adjusted and surrender cost indexes after 5, 10, and 20 years?
7. What's the loan rate?
8. Is there direct recognition?
9. What's the insurance company's financial ratings by A.M. Best? How do either Standard & Poor's, Moody's, or Duff and Phelps rate the firm's claims-paying ability?

POINTS TO REMEMBER

- Variable life insurance is for people who can understand and accept the risks and rewards of investing in stocks and bonds.
- Variable life insurance policyholders have a choice of different types of mutual funds to invest their cash value. The policyholders direct their investments and bear the risk.
- You have a choice of common stock mutual funds to invest your cash value. Aggressive stock funds are the riskiest type of mutual funds. These funds invest in small company growth stocks. Growth and income funds are less risky because they invest in high-yield blue chip stocks. Income funds invest in high-dividend-yield stocks.
- You also have a choice of bond funds to pick from in a variable life insurance policy. Junk bond funds pay high yields, but invest in poor-credit-rated companies. Funds that invest in investment grade bonds own the most creditworthy corporate securities. You can also invest in government bond funds backed directly or indirectly by the U.S. government against default. The bond funds also invest in different maturities. You can invest in funds that invest in bonds with maturities of 20 to 30 years or funds that invest in bonds with maturities of 1 to 10 years. The long-term bond funds pay higher yields than short-term bond funds, but the long-term bond funds have greater price volatility when interest rates rise.
- You can also invest in an account in your variable life insurance policy that pays a fixed rate guaranteed by the insurance company.
- You can buy a single premium variable life insurance policy and make just one payment for your coverage. Or you can pay level premiums for the insurance coverage.
- Your death benefits are tied to the performance of your mutual fund investments. However, the insurance company guarantees you will receive the face amount of coverage you initially purchased.

- You can borrow against the cash value of your variable life insurance policy. The insurance company, however, will put the cash value equal to the loan amount in a fixed rate investment account.
- Financial planners say that variable life insurance policyholders should diversify their investments. If they split their investments among common stocks, bonds, and money funds, they will have less volatile returns with the least amount of risk.

10

Annuities

Annuities are a good alternative for people who want to have some extra cash at retirement or are looking for a tax-deferred investment alternative to CDs.

Annuities are one of the hottest selling investment products on the market today. According to the Life Insurance Marketing and Research Association (LIMRA), annuity sales were up 22 percent in 1991. Sales increased to almost $60 billion in 1990 from $25 billion in 1986. LIMRA reports that most purchasers are married people between 30 and 60 years old. They tend to work in the professions or hold managerial positions. Mostly, they earn less than $50,000 per year. LIMRA attributes the growth in annuity sales to the interest by consumers in spending more money on living benefits such as retirement and health care rather than life insurance death benefits.

WHAT IS AN ANNUITY?

An annuity is a contract with a life insurance company that requires you to make a lump sum or periodic payments in an account that earns tax-deferred interest until funds are withdrawn. You receive income from the investment based on the payout option you select. When you start getting a monthly check from your annuity, you are *annuitizing* the contract.

Only that part of the annuity income that represents investment earnings is subject to federal taxes. You don't pay tax on that part of the distributions representing your original payments. Each annuity payment is taxed proportionately, based on the value of the annuity and the premiums paid.

DIFFERENT KINDS OF ANNUITIES

Annuities, like many insurance products, come in several forms. Some are designed as long-term savings vehicles. Others pay immediately. In addition, you can buy annuities that pay fixed or variable rates. For example:

- *Deferred Annuities.* You make a lump sum or periodic payments into an annuity. After age 59½, you can begin taking distributions without penalty from the insurance company or the IRS. Deferred annuities are considered a way to supplement retirement savings. It's a type of forced savings plan with a tax-deferred kicker. Several types of deferred annuities are available:
  - —Periodic payments to an annuity that pays a fixed rate of interest that can be adjusted at set times (e.g., annually, or every 3 to 5 years).
  - —Fixed-rate, single-premium, deferred annuity where you make a lump-sum payment of $5,000 or more.

  Rudy Watz, CLU, ChFC, and vice president with Value Securities, New York, stresses, "Fixed annuities are most appropriate for conservative savers who want the assurance of a guaranteed rate of return on their money that grows tax deferred."
- *Deferred Variable Annuities.* You make periodic payments or a lump-sum payment into an annuity with a variety of stock and bond mutual funds. The advantage, according to Watz: You control your investment decisions. If you are willing to assume risk, you can attain higher returns over the long term.

In addition to the potential for long-term gains, your money is invested in a variable annuity separate account. The assets in a variable annuity are not subject to any of the insurance company's creditors' claims.

- *Immediate Annuities.* You invest a lump sum and receive payments immediately over your lifetime. When you die, your beneficiaries will inherit the balance of the money, if you elected the appropriate payout option when you signed the annuity contract. Deferred annuities become immediate annuities when you decide to start taking payments.

Chapter 13 discusses the different types of payout or settlement options for both life insurance and annuity policyholders.

How much should I invest in an annuity?

There are two types of annuity investors—those who want to make a lump-sum tax-deferred investment for the long term and those who put money away every month. In addition to the tax-deferred feature, though, one of the biggest advantages of an annuity is that you generally don't have to begin taking money out until age 85. That's a big plus compared with Individual Retirement Accounts (IRAs), where you have to start taking money out by the time you reach 70½ years of age or you get hit with stiff fines from the IRS: 50 percent of the difference between what you take out and what's required by law.

People are living longer today. So that means you could get an extra 10 years of tax-deferred income from an annuity compared with an IRA. Say, for example, you had a $100,000 savings kitty at age 70. Over the next 10 years you could more than double your money tax-free in an annuity. If you earned 8 percent a year on that money, your stash would grow to $215,900.

How much should I put in an annuity?

Assuming you need a side fund at retirement, here is how much you would save investing $1,500 a year into an annuity that grew at an annual rate of 8 percent. Also assume you are in the 28 percent tax bracket.

- Over 5 years, the money would grow to $10,073.
- Over 10 years, the money would grow to $26,297.
- Over 20 years, the money would grow to $95,504.
- Over 30 years, the money would grow to $271,415.

THE DOWNSIDE

There is no free lunch when you invest in annuities. First, the rate you earn on a fixed-rate annuity could decline after a couple of years. You pay a lot of fees when you first buy a variable type annuity. You pay administrative charges, maybe a state premium tax, mortality fees, and back-end surrender charges if you cash the policy out early. In addition, the IRS will assess a 10 percent fine if you are under age 59½ and take money out of any type of annuity.

Later on in this chapter, a section highlights the basic tax rules on annuities. Tax laws, however, are subject to change, so consult your financial advisor before you act.

THE PROS AND CONS OF DIFFERENT TYPES OF ANNUITIES

Not all annuities are alike. There are pros and cons to buying single premium, flexible premium fixed rate, and/or variable rate annuities.

When you buy a fixed rate annuity, the insurance company pays you interest based on the performance of their investments. Say for example, that all the assets of the insurance company earned a total of 9 percent for the year: After the company subtracts out the cost of doing business and the margin for profit, it may pay you 7 percent.

Variable annuities are different because you control investments. If you own a variable annuity, you invest the money in a stable of mutual funds that are placed in a separate account from the insurance company's pool of assets. Your mutual fund returns will be based on how the stock and bond markets perform.

Single Premium Fixed Rate Annuities

THE PROS. The investment grows tax deferred until you make withdrawals. When interest rates are high, you can lock in a lump sum at a guaranteed rate of interest for up to 10 years. The back-end surrender charge declines every year, usually for 7 years. After that time, you can withdraw funds without paying a back-end exit fee.

THE CONS. Inflation can eat away at the purchasing power of your money that is earning a fixed rate of interest. Your investment is a direct obligation of the insurance company. The assets of the insurance company are subject to creditors' claims. That means you could receive less than you expected if your investment with a financially troubled insurance company is acquired by another firm.

Flexible Premium Fixed Rate Annuities

THE PROS. This type of annuity is affordable. You make periodic payments over the years. So you have a forced savings plan. The money grows tax deferred until you take distributions after age 59½.

THE CONS. Since you earn a fixed rate, the value of your investment is affected by inflation. In addition, every payment you make is tied to a back-end surrender charge. You end up paying a level back-end surrender charge on a flexible premium annuity. You pay the same fee over at least 7 years. The back-end charge rate does not drop over time, except on older payments—those more than 7 years old.

Single Premium Variable Annuities

THE PROS. The money grows tax deferred. You can invest in a choice of common stock and bond funds. Historically, stock funds have grown at an annual rate of 10 percent over the past 6 decades. You pay a back-end surrender charge that declines over 7 years.

THE CONS. The stock market is risky. There is more price volatility over the short term when you invest in the stock market.

Flexible Premium Variable Annuities

THE PROS. The money grows tax deferred until you withdraw funds. You can make an initial investment of as little as $1,000 and $100 subsequent investments. You participate in the long-term growth of the stock market. It's a forced savings plan. By investing $100 a month, for example, you can dollar cost average your stock fund investment. The cons are the same as the single premium variable annuity.

WEALTH BUILDING PROFILE ***Retirement Savings.*** Bernard, age 45, needs to supplement his retirement savings. His financial planner conducted a retirement needs analysis and found out that the psychologist needs about $100,000 to supplement his Keogh plan and Social Security income. So Ben is investing $235 a month in a variable annuity. He has one-third of his money invested in a common stock, bond, and money fund. Over the long term, he estimates his money will grow at an 8 percent annual rate tax-free. And by the time he reaches age 65, he will have accumulated $100,000. That side fund will provide him with $556 of monthly income for the next 20 years.

TAKING PAYMENTS FROM YOUR ANNUITY

There are several distribution options to pick from: Life income option, a life income option with a lump-sum payout to your beneficiaries, and a joint and survivor option. With a life income option, you receive income for as long as you live. The payouts are higher than with the other options. The big drawback is that your beneficiaries do not collect anything when you die. The insurance company keeps the balance of your account.

Another option is called "life income and certain," which ranges from 5 to 20 years. You get lifetime income from the life and certain annuity payment. The monthly payment is lower than the life income option. However, when you die, your beneficiaries inherit all the money that's left in the annuity. If you die during the terms of the life income and certain payout plan, your beneficiaries continue to receive income for a specific number of years. For example, suppose Tom dies with three years left on his 15-year life and certain contract: His beneficiaries get the remaining income over three years.

The "life income and certain" option can be set up so that the beneficiaries will receive a lump sum of the remaining money in the annuity, rather than get monthly payments. This is known as a "cash refund" annuity.

Under a joint and survivor option, you get income for your lifetime. When you die, your spouse gets income for his or her lifetime. The payout to the surviving spouse is usually reduced 50 percent.

Can I withdraw some of the money out of my deferred annuity?

If you are under 59½ years of age, you will have to pay a 10 percent federal excise tax and ordinary income tax on the earnings component of the withdrawal. Most insurance companies let you withdraw 10 percent of your contributions or 10 percent of the value of the annuity free of the back-end surrender charge or load. See an overview of the annuity tax rules at the end of the chapter.

FINDING A LOW-COST VARIABLE ANNUITY

Most fixed rate annuities charge no up-front commissions or fees. The insurance company takes its cut out of the investment income. If you earn 7 percent on an annuity, the insurance company may be making 9 percent or more. In addition, if you take money out of the annuity, you may get charged a lower rate than stated when you signed the contract. Not only that, you will pay a back-end surrender charge on withdrawals over a fixed number of years. The surrender charge disappears or vanishes after a specified time period.

The earnings on either the fixed or variable annuity aren't taxed until distributions are received. However, variable annuities can cost more than fixed rate annuities, because of the additional charges attached to such plans. Besides the back-end surrender charge, you must pay a mutual fund management fee, a mortality fee (about 2 percent a year), and an administrative charge. On average, the fees total 2 percent, according to VARDs, a Miami, FL, annuity reporting service.

ACTION ITEM

When shopping for a variable annuity, check the product's prospectus. The Securities and Exchange Commission requires that the expense table in the prospectus list all expenses up front in three sections: one detailing transaction expenses such as sales loads, surrender fees, and exchange fees; the second listing annual fees; and the third detailing annual mutual fund management fees, mortality, and expense fees.

ACTION ITEM

Look at the fee section in the annuity's prospectus. You will see an example that shows you what $1,000 grows to at a 5 percent annual return after fees are deducted. Compare annuities and pick the product with the lowest expenses and the best performing mutual funds over at least a 3- to 5-year period.

ACTION ITEM

Fees can eat into your variable annuity's mutual fund returns. The Scudder Horizon Plan and the Vanguard Variable Annuity Plan are two of the lowest cost products on the market. Scudder's operating expenses are 1.31 percent. Vanguard's operating expenses are 1 percent. Neither plan has a back-end surrender charge. For more information, call Scudder at 800-225-2470 and Vanguard at 800-662-7447.

COMBINATION ANNUITIES

If you are about to retire and want monthly income plus a tax-deferred investment, you might consider buying a split-funded or combination annuity. That means you buy an immediate annuity and a deferred annuity at the same time. You get income from the immediate annuity, for a set period of time, say 5 or 10 years. After the funds from the immediate annuity are depleted, payments come from the cash that has accumulated in the deferred annuity.

"A combination annuity is for people who want income and preservation of principal," says Michael Burk, president of Anderson Burk, Inc., a Seattle-based research firm. "Not only are you guaranteed to get the original deposit amount back at the end of the cycle, but the income is guaranteed as well."

This type of annuity can be advantageous because it avoids this problem: Say you have $100,000 to invest and want monthly income. Here's what would happen if you put the entire $100,000 in an immediate annuity that pays you income for 10 years: (1) All the money would be used up over time; (2) you would have to pay income tax on that part of your immediate annuity payment that represents investment earnings; and (3) you are also locked into the insurance company's rate for 10 years. If rates rise, you lose potential income.

WEALTH BUILDING PROFILE *Split-Fund Annuity.* Anne, age 68, decided to do a split-fund annuity. Her financial planner explained how she could get current income and a tax-deferred investment at the same time. She invested $100,000.

Anne put $68,058 in a deferred annuity that paid 8 percent annual interest for 5 years. At the end of 5 years, the money will have grown to $100,000.

The remaining $31,942 was put into a 5-year immediate annuity. At current rates, she receives $633 income each month for five years. Only $99 a month—or 16 percent of that amount—is taxed. The rest of the money is not taxed because it is considered principal.

At the end of the 5-year period, there is no money left in the immediate annuity. However, Anne still has $100,000; the $68,058 in the deferred annuity and $31,942 in tax-deferred interest income.

ACTION ITEM

Inflation will erode the purchasing power of your second annuity. Even though you have the same dollar amount at the end of that time, you will have less purchasing power. You may be able to earn more after-tax interest income from a corporate bond fund or tax-free municipal bond fund.

BE LEERY OF DEATH BENEFIT GUARANTEES

Many annuity owners afraid of losing money in a stock market plunge are switching into annuities with extended death benefit guarantees. These policies guarantee that your heirs will get 100 percent of the original principal invested in the annuity in the event of your death. It looks like a great deal on the surface, but you really aren't getting very much. The insurance company has to pay only if the stock market plunges at the same time an annuity owner dies.

Variable annuities issued several years ago have death benefit protection up to age 75. Many newer policies maintain coverage to age 85 or longer. Insurance companies decided to extend the death benefit coverage to make their new annuity products more attractive to potential customers. Many newer policies maintain coverage to 85 years or longer.

"It's a sales gimmick and marketing ploy," says Hubert Mueller, actuarial consultant at Tillinghast in New York.

"Brokers and agents are selling the extended death benefits to get higher commissions." Mueller adds that time is on the side of the insurance companies because people that buy annuities are healthier and live longer than people who take out insurance policies. Death benefits are a no-lose proposition for the insurance company.

CD ANNUITIES

Many people who are looking for a more traditional vehicle look at high-yield certificates of annuities that pay fixed rates higher than bank CDs for term to maturities of usually one, two, or three years. Investors lock into higher rates than those of tax-deferred CDs. After the CD term expires, though, the insurance company will pay a much lower rate for the rolled-over CD.

HIGH YIELDS THAT ARE SAFE AND TAX-FREE

If you can afford a long-term investment, consider certificates of annuities.

Financially strong insurance companies aren't giving away the store. But at the time of this writing, you could lock into 5 to 7 percent tax-free for 1 to 10 years in an annuity. The rates, however, will be reset after the term of the deal is over. In addition, you have to tie your money up until you reach age 59½ or you pay early withdrawal penalties. The IRS hits you with income tax and a 10 percent fine. In addition, annuities have back-end surrender charges. That's a back-end redemption fee lasting 5 to 10 years.

When you take distributions after 59½ years of age, only that part of your distribution that represents investment earnings is taxed, not your principal.

You can earn up to 7 percent tax deferred for up to 10 years from A+ best-rate insurance companies that also have triple A claims-paying ratings.

For example, at the time of this writing, you could get satisfactory tax-deferred rates from the following financially strong insurance companies:

- Lincoln Benefit Life Company is paying 4 percent on a 1-year annuity CD. This firm is rated A+ for financial strength by A.M. Best and carries a triple A claims-paying rating by Standard & Poor's.
- Metropolitan Life is paying 5.5 percent for 1 year and 5.35 percent on a 5-year annuity. The insurance company has an A+ Best rating and triple A ratings from Standard & Poor's, Moody's, and Duff & Phelps.
- Hartford Life Insurance company is paying 5.1 percent on a 3-year CD annuity, 6.5 percent for 6 years, and 6.65 percent for 7 years. The firm is rated A+ by Best and carries triple A claims-paying ratings from Standard & Poor's and Duff & Phelps.

FIXED-RATE ANNUITIES VERSUS MUNICIPAL BONDS

Should you invest supplemental retirement savings or your lump-sum pension withdrawals in tax-free municipal bonds or a tax-sheltered annuity that promises to pay you income over the long term?

ACTION ITEM

Talk to your financial advisor before you invest any lump sum. You could put money into a tax-free investment or annuity at the wrong time. You might invest in bonds and then find interest rates rising and the market value of your investment declining. Or you could lock into a fixed-rate annuity only to find rates rising a week later.

ACTION ITEM

Weigh the pluses and minuses of your tax-free investment options before you invest. Your age, income, health, tax status, and your existing investments all play a factor when it comes to salting away your hard-earned money in municipal bonds or annuities.

Recent research indicates that high-tax bracket investors seeking long-term tax-free income might be better off investing in an annuity rather than a municipal bond.

According to a study written by Richard Toolson, assistant accounting professor at Washington State University, Pullman, WA ("The Nonqualified Annuity: A Viable Tax Shelter," *Journal of Taxation of Investments,* Warren Gorham & Lamont, 1989), found that the pretax returns on annuities are a better deal than municipal bonds for those who are salting away money until retirement.

"Generally, exempt securities have a tax advantage over nonqualified annuities in that the interest earned is permanently excluded from income (not merely deferred) and is not subject to a premature withdrawal penalty," said Toolson. "Because of this, issuers of exempt securities can offer a lower interest rate than issuers of nonqualified annuities. [But] lengthening the period of accumulation [in an annuity] taking distributions when the annuitant is in a lower tax bracket, and avoiding premature withdrawal penalties will increase the effective after-tax rate of return on annuities."

Toolson compared the returns on a $1,000 initial investment in a municipal bond that earned 7 percent to maturity, assuming reinvestment of interest and annual compounding, with an annuity for the same holding period. In addition, a determination was made of the pretax rate of return an annuity would have to earn to have the same accrued value as the municipal bond, including the tax consequences of cashing in the annuity.

He also assumed no transaction costs were involved because there are no-load munibond funds and annuities with just back-end surrender charges on the market today.

The results of his study revealed that as the holding period of the annuity increases, the break-even rate decreases; that is, there is a decrease in the pretax rate of return the annuity needs to earn to equal the same after-tax value as the 7.5 percent municipal bond. For example, the study showed that a taxpayer in the 28 percent bracket who held an annuity for 5 years would have to earn 11.2 percent on his investment to break even with the municipal bond. The break-even rate would drop to 10.4 percent for a 10-year holding period, 9.9 percent for a 15-year holding period, and 9.5 percent for a 20-year holding period.

However, if the annuitant intends to hold the investment for the long term and avoid the 10 percent early withdrawal penalty, the break-even rates are reduced. Assuming the same 7.5 percent tax-free earnings on the municipal bond, a person who held the annuity for 5 years and had a distribution period of 5 years would need to earn 9.8 percent before taxes to break even. The break-even rate on a 10-year holding and distribution period would be 9.2 percent. And a 20-year holding period and 10-year distribution period would break even with the munibond at a rate of 8.7 percent.

ANNUITY TAX BENEFITS

- The interest or earnings on annuity investments are tax deferred until you take distributions.
- If you take money out of an annuity issued after August 13, 1982, before you reach age 59½, the interest earnings on the annuity are taxable income and you must pay a 10

percent early withdrawal fine on the amount includable in gross income.

- You can take regular withdrawals in substantially equal payments over your lifetime from your annuity before you turn age 59½ without incurring the 10 percent fine. However, you must pay the federal taxes, unless you are over age 59½ and have taken the payouts for at least 5 years.
- You don't have to pay the early withdrawal fine if you become totally or permanently disabled and need the money. Distributions due to death are not fined.
- You can swap your old annuity for a new one with better features tax-free by making a "Section 1035 exchange." Get professional advice before making this switch.
- When the annuity owner dies, payments must be made to any nonspouse beneficiaries within 5 years, or over the life expectancy of the beneficiary. Payments, however, must begin no later than December 31 after the year the person died. If the beneficiary is the spouse, he or she can become owner of the policy and does not have to worry about the payout rules involving others.
- If you bought an annuity after August 13, 1982, and pledge the annuity as collateral for a loan, the IRS considers this action a cash withdrawal. That means you pay taxes and possibly a 10 percent early withdrawal fine.
- During any calendar year after October 21, 1988, if you buy the same type of annuity from the same insurance company, the IRS considers this one annuity contract for tax purposes. For example, if you own two deferred annuities from XZY insurance company, the IRA views this as one annuity. Or if you own two immediate annuities from the same insurance company, it's considered one immediate annuity when you do your income tax. However, if you own both a deferred annuity and an immediate annuity from the same insurance company, the IRS rule does not apply.

POINTS TO REMEMBER

- Annuities are considered a supplementary source of retirement savings along with a pension plan or IRA.
- Deferred annuities are contracts with insurance companies that you pay for in either a lump sum or in periodic payments over the long term. The insurance company promises to pay you income for your lifetime when you retire.
- Immediate annuities pay you income over your lifetime right away. They are purchased by retired people who want a secure source of income.
- As with IRAs, the earnings on annuities are tax deferred. But you don't get a tax deduction for making contributions to annuities. By contrast, you can contribute as much as you want to an annuity. IRAs are limited to $2,000 of earned income for singles and $4,000 for those married and filing jointly, if a person doesn't have a company pension plan.
- You can begin taking distributions from an annuity at any time after you turn 59½ years of age and before you reach age 85.
- Fixed annuities pay you a fixed rate of interest on your investment. The rate is determined by how the insurance company invests its assets.
- With variable annuities, you can invest your payments in a stable of common stock and bond mutual funds.
- Despite the performance of your variable annuity mutual funds, the insurance company will pay you a guaranteed rate on your annuity.
- You can take a tax deduction for payments to an IRA. But when you retire and take distributions, you pay income tax on the money.
- Consult a financial planner before you purchase an annuity. An annuity should be part of an overall financial game plan. You should also have a will, disability, life insurance, and a retirement savings plan.

11

Diversifying Your Variable Life and Annuity Mutual Fund Portfolios

Can you do better than your insurance company's illustrated 7 to 8 percent rate it pays on the cash value of your whole life policy?

The answer is a qualified yes. If you have investment experience, are comfortable managing your own money, and know a lot about how the financial markets work, then a variable life or annuity policy may be right for you.

They call these policies variable products for a good reason. The value of the investment changes as financial conditions change. When business prospects look good, corporate profits rise and so do stock prices. A recession is generally bad for stocks because company profits decline and people get laid off at work. Conversely, high inflation eats away at the value of money, so interest rates have to rise to compensate investors for a loss of purchasing power. Bond prices move in opposite directions to interest rates. So rising interest rates result in falling bond prices. But when the economy slows, interest rates decline and bond prices rise.

Historically, according to Ibbotson & Associates statistics, stocks have grown at an annual rate of 10 percent a year. But in any given year, you can see a 21 percent swing in price from the average. You could be up 31 percent one year and down 11 percent or more the next.

Government bonds also show price volatility. Over the past 60 years, bonds have grown at an annual rate of 5 percent with a price swing of 6 percent. In any given year, based on past history, you could expect a return ranging from −1 percent to 11 percent in long-term Treasury bonds. More recently, however, bonds have shown much greater volatility. You are getting price swings of more than 8 percent.

By investing in a variable life policy, you can ride along with the fortunes of the economy. That may not sound too inviting. Over the long term, however, if you invest in the stock market, you should make much more than you would with CDs or bonds.

Variable life lets you get in on the action. Insurance companies offer you a choice of investing in a stable of stocks, bonds, and money market funds. Some variable life policies also have funds that invest worldwide or in precious metals as an inflation hedge.

ADVANTAGES AND DISADVANTAGES OF VARIABLE ANNUITIES

There are several advantages to putting your money in a variable annuity. There are drawbacks, too.

The Good News

Your variable life insurance investments are not a direct obligation of the insurance company. You are a bondholder or stockholder in a portfolio of securities. Mutual funds pool investors' money and diversify their portfolios in a large number of issuers or industries. That way, if a few securities perform poorly, gains in other securities may offset your losses.

When you get a fixed rate that's paid to you directly by the insurance company, you sink or swim with the fortunes of the company. If the insurance company's earnings and profits are down, you will get paid less or receive less in dividends than you expected.

If an insurance company goes under and is taken over by state regulators and is merged, you have to settle for lower than expected returns. For example, in the early 1980s when interest rates were at 12 percent, Baldwin United's policyholders had to accept a 7.5 percent rate after the company was acquired by a larger insurance company.

Second, you can tailor your portfolio based on your tolerance for risk and economic expectations. A later section in this chapter explains how you can diversify your variable insurance investments.

Now the Bad News

If you don't know what you are doing and put all your money in an aggressive stock fund, you could see the value of the investment drop 25 percent in any given year. Or you could put too much in bonds and money funds. If you are too conservative, you can miss out on some long-term profits. You might earn less than the whole life policy rate.

WHAT MUTUAL FUNDS DO FOR YOU

Mutual funds are a diversified way to build your wealth. You get three layers of protection when you invest in mutual funds.

Mutual funds pool a large number of investors' money and buy a large number of securities. The funds are professionally managed and diversified. If a few stocks do poorly because of bad news about a few companies, the losses are washed out by gains from other stocks in the mutual fund portfolio.

You get another layer of protection when you diversify your mutual fund investments. Stock, bond, and cash investment prices usually don't move in tandem. If stocks are down, bonds may be up. If bonds are down, stocks may be up. Likewise, overseas stock and bond prices generally don't move in tandem with the U.S. securities markets. Therefore, losses in stocks here at home might be offset by gains in overseas financial markets. In addition, a money fund keeps a value of $1 per share, serving as an anchor to the portfolio.

You have a couple of pairs of steel-belted investments to protect you from a blowout. If the stock fund is down, the bond fund might be up. Or your overseas equity fund could be showing large gains. And the more money you put into a money fund, the less you will lose when your stock or bond fund drops in price.

TYPES OF MUTUAL FUNDS: A FUND FOR ALL SEASONS

Mutual funds are what variable insurance products are all about. Mutual funds come in different varieties based on risk and investment objectives. With over 3,000 mutual funds on the market, some say there's a mutual fund for all seasons. Individuals can match their level of risk and investment goals with the mutual fund objectives. While no two mutual funds are exactly alike, they fall into several broad-based categories.

Aggressive Growth Funds

These are the riskiest equity funds. The funds seek maximum capital appreciation and provide little current income to investors. Typically, the funds invest in new companies or existing growth companies that are traded on the over-the-counter stock market. The funds may also invest in companies or industries that are out of favor, regardless of capitalization because of the profit potential in undervalued or overlooked stocks. Other aggressive growth funds will invest in any size company that shows strong profit potential.

In the 1960s, aggressive stock funds were called "go-go" funds. Today, things haven't changed. These funds have the ability to outperform the market by as much as 25 to 60 percent. On the downside, however, investors can lose just as much if the portfolio manager's stock selection is wrong or the overall market is in a steep decline.

Growth Funds

Like their aggressive cousins, growth funds look for capital appreciation. They are, however, less risky because the funds invest in well-seasoned companies that also pay dividends. Income from a growth fund is a secondary consideration. For example, Janus Fund, up 18.5 percent annually over the past 15 years, currently yields just 1.2 percent. But the fund owns such blue chip stocks as Merck, American Express, and Boeing. For growth, it has a stake in fast-growing companies such as Wal-Mart, a rapidly expanding retailer, and MCI Communications, an over-the-counter telephone company.

Growth funds can run neck and neck with aggressive stock funds in the performance ratings. The funds on average have grown at an annual rate of 15 percent over the past 15 years, 12 percent over the past 10 years, and 9 percent over the past 5 years.

Growth and Income Funds

These funds invest in well-seasoned blue chip companies that have a track record of paying dividends. Some funds call themselves Equity Income Funds. But there's not much difference between the two groups. Both spot high dividend yields and focus on total return.

These funds are less risky than the growth-oriented funds because they invest in larger capitalized companies that have the cash flow to pay shareholders bigger dividends. And those dividends serve to cushion the blow from stock market declines. Over the past 15 years, these funds, on average, have grown at an annual rate of 14 percent. But the funds are about 25 percent less volatile than the S&P 500.

Balanced Funds

These all-weather funds focus on preservation of principal. A balanced fund will invest in a mixed portfolio with a fixed percentage in common stock, preferred stock, and bonds. Balanced funds are less volatile than the S&P 500 or the Dow Jones Industrial Average. Investors receive income from high-yielding equities and fixed-income securities. Balanced funds will generally underperform in a bull market in stocks, but outperform the market during a recession.

Total return funds, a hybrid form of a balanced fund, give investors the opportunity for more profit potential. Total return portfolio managers have greater flexibility than balanced fund managers. They can use market timing to move between stocks and fixed income securities in any percentage they choose when investment conditions change.

Income Funds

These funds seek a high level of current income for shareholders by investing in high-dividend-paying common stock, preferred stock, and government and corporate bonds. The funds can be considered a more growth-oriented substitute for balance funds. But since a large part of their return is due to interest and dividend income, the funds are more sensitive than other stock funds to changes in interest rates. So if interest rates rise, the fund's portfolio value will decline.

The funds also hold solid long-term growth stocks such as Texaco, NYNEX, AT&T, and Johnson & Johnson. According to Lipper Analytical Services, New York, income funds can invest up to 60 percent in equities and up to 75 percent in bonds.

Income funds currently yield between 5 and 9 percent. The Income Fund of America, for example, is yielding 6 percent and is about 40 percent invested in stocks. The fund, however, looks for capital growth and has grown at an annual rate of 13 percent over the past 15 years.

Bond Funds

Bond funds have several investment objectives. Some invest in long-term bonds, others in intermediate and short-term notes. Some bond funds invest in only the most creditworthy issuers—those companies whose debt obligations are rated A to triple A by Standard & Poor's and Moody's. Low-rated issuers pay higher yields because there is a greater risk of default during economic recessions. Bonds rated BB or lower are called junk bonds. Currently, mutual funds that invest in junk bonds are yielding almost 10 percent or almost 3.5 percent more than Treasury securities because investors are being compensated for greater risks.

There are also bond funds that invest in government securities. Funds that invest solely in U.S. Treasury securities carry no credit risk or default risk because the bonds are backed by the "full faith and credit" of the government. Securities funds also invest in U.S. government agency debt obligations. These funds invest primarily in Federal Home Loan Bank Board bonds, and in Government National Mortgage Association, Federal National Mortgage Association, and Federal Home Loan Mortgage Corporation bonds.

Government security bond funds usually pay about ½ percent more than Treasury bonds for several reasons. First, U.S. government agency debt carries an implied moral obligation, not a full faith and credit obligation, that the federal government will back up any defaults. Second, many government agencies issue mortgage bonds. As a result, both principal and interest is paid off to investors during the lifetime of the bond. Government mortgage bond funds reinvest the principal and may distribute the interest to investors.

Because of repayment of both principal and interest, which would have to be reinvested at a rate not comparable to the original bond issue, the marketplace demands higher yields on these bonds. Currently, for example, GNMA mortgage bonds are yielding about 8 percent compared with 7 percent on long-term Treasury bonds.

Bond funds are not without risk. Although there is generally a low correlation between bond and equity returns, bond funds can be just as volatile as stocks. Bond prices move in opposite directions to interest rates. When interest rates rise, bond prices fall. In addition, the longer the maturity of the bond, the greater the price volatility.

Money Market Funds

Money funds invest in short-term money market instruments with less than 270 days to maturity. They invest in T-bills, certificates of deposit, commercial paper, and repurchase agreements that are over 100 percent collateralized. Since the funds are required to carry an average maturity of less than 125 days, they can maintain an unchanging net asset value of $1 per share. There is no price volatility with money funds, but you earn lower yields. Money funds also have check-writing privileges and can be used by corporate treasurers to concentrate daily cash balances or to pay bills. The safest money funds are in Treasury bills and notes and other U.S. government agency obligations. The funds that pay the highest yields are invested in money center bank CDs and commercial paper—IOUs of top credit-rated corporations.

Overseas Mutual Funds

These funds come in two forms. Global funds can invest in both the U.S. and overseas stock markets. International funds exclude the U.S. stocks and bonds from their portfolios. These funds are attractive because they offer an extra layer of diversification to mutual fund holdings. Many of the world's stock markets lead or lag the U.S. market. As a result, losses in U.S. holdings may be offset by gains overseas. You can also invest in overseas bond funds. Foreign mutual funds, however, carry additional risks. Changes in the value of the dollar in relation to other currencies can affect the market value of overseas holdings. Investors also face political risks and must contend with volatility of the indigenous markets.

Precious metals mutual funds, however, are often considered a long-term inflation hedge. Financial planners often recommend that investors keep 5 percent of their assets in precious metals. When inflation rises, bonds and stocks get hit hard, but gold and gold-related assets appreciate and balance out an investor's wealth.

There are caveats to investing in precious metals funds. Over the 5 years ending in January 1992, precious metals mutual funds have grown at a − 1.6 percent. And over 10 years, these funds have grown at an annual rate of just 3.5 percent. As long as inflation stays low, there is always a danger of investing in a long-term inflation hedge. Consult your financial advisor before you invest in precious metals to make sure you are doing the right thing.

YOU NEED A BRIDGE OVER TROUBLED WATERS

Let's get more specific about diversification. Many financial planners say that it's best to split up your variable life insurance investments, at least among stocks, bonds, and cash. What risks are you reducing when you diversify? You face several risks when you invest in the financial markets. Let's look at the risks closely to see how diversification will protect your principal. You might lost money when you diversify. But you will limit the decline in the market value of your hard-earned investments.

- *Nonmarket Risk.* That's the risk that a firm's stock or bond price could tumble because of bad news about the company, the economy, or some type of management crisis. Say the third-quarter earnings report on XYZ Widgets shows a drop in profitability compared with the preceding year. The price of stock is liable to drop because investors sell. Or suppose Standard & Poor's and Moody's downgrade the credit rating on a firm's bond issues. The bond prices will tumble. Or what happens if the CEO dies unexpectedly? Nervous investors are prone to sell.

  If you own just a few stocks or bonds, you lose on bad news. But if you hold a portfolio of at least 25 stocks, financial research shows you will minimize the nonmarket risk. Losses in a few issues won't hurt the overall performance of your portfolio. And that's one way mutual funds limit losses. They own a large number of stocks in different industries.

- *Market Risk.* Financial research also shows us that almost 60 percent of a stock or bond's price is determined by the market. So if the S&P 500 is up, there's a good chance your AAA corporate bond's price is up. But there is always a good chance of exposure on the downside.

ACTION ITEM

You can minimize the risk of owning stocks here at home by investing in other assets such as overseas stock and bond mutual funds. The reason: Different types of assets perform differently. So you may get protection if almost all U.S. stocks decline and your international mutual fund holds its ground or loses less.

- *Purchasing Power Risk.* If inflation grows 5 percent a year for 14 years, it will cost you about $200 for your $100 grocery bill today. To protect yourself against the ravages of inflation, some money managers keep part of the investment in precious metals, real estate, and stocks. Over the long term, these assets have historically given about a 3 percent return over the rate of inflation.
- *Bond Market Risk.* You face interest rate risk. When interest rates rise, bond prices fall. The longer the maturity of the bond, the greater the price fluctuation. You also face event or default risk. If business is bad, a firm may default on its interest and principal payments.

DIVERSIFICATION SAVED MONEY DURING THE 1987 CRASH

What happened during the October 1987 stock market crash is a good example of how diversification works. Stock and bond prices swung crazily. On October 19, 1987, the stock market dropped 500 points, fell 40 percent from its high, and closed out the year with a measly gain of only 2 percent. Subsequently, the stock market rebounded, gaining back about two-thirds of its losses at the time of this writing. This rebound affords small consolation to the many investors who, attracted by soaring returns, bought stocks at the end of August and lost 28 percent by the end of October. Those nearing retirement who had most of their money in equities saw a third of their future income evaporate before they sold, in a blind panic to avoid losing everything.

On the other hand, some savvy investors managed to escape the repercussions of the market plunge. Those who diversified, keeping just a third of their portfolios in stocks, bonds, or cash, weathered the stock shock. For example, from August 20, 1987 through October 29, 1987, the S&P 500 dropped 27 percent. But a person who had 33 percent of his or her assets in growth stocks, bonds, and money market mutual funds would have lost only 9 percent during that period. Those with some overseas bond funds in their portfolio lost about 6 percent during that same time frame.

THE 1990 STOCK MARKET CORRECTION

The 1990 stock market pullback is another recent example of how stashing your cash in a diversified portfolio of mutual funds can save you lots of money.

In August through September 1990, some aggressive growth stock funds lost 30 percent. If you invested a large part of your savings in the hopes of getting rich quick, you are a lot poorer today. But if you diversified in stocks, bonds, and cash, you were up about 5 to 6 percent year to date, ending in the third quarter of 1990, compared with an 11 percent decline in the S&P 500. By the end of the third quarter of 1990, after Iraq invaded Kuwait, the average U.S. stock fund dropped 13 percent. Equity funds that were invested worldwide were down about the same. However, money funds were paying about 7 percent and global funds appreciated 8 percent in value.

OVER TEN YEARS, DIVERSIFICATION WORKED

How did diversified portfolios perform during the 1980s compared with individual investments? According to Salomon Brothers data, a diversified portfolio of securities grew at an annual rate of 13 percent over that decade. Stocks grew at a phenomenal rate of 18 percent a year; bonds, 13 percent; real estate, 12 percent; and money market funds, 9 percent. Though you earned less money in a diversified portfolio, your risks were half as much as 100 percent position in stocks.

The lesson: When you diversify your investments, you reduce risk and get a comfortable return.

YOUR RISKS AND MIX OF MUTUAL FUNDS

The only thing you can't do with your portfolio is divide it up and forget about it. Your risk level may change. You may also want to make a practice of rebalancing your portfolio annually so that it stays in line with your investment philosophy. That way, you'll never have too much money at risk. If your stocks have gone up 25 percent in value, for instance, and now represent half of your portfolio, you may want to shift some of the profits into bonds and money funds.

What counts is the mix: getting and keeping the right investment formula. As in fine baking, if you put in the right amount of quality ingredients, you'll usually be satisfied with the results.

The Risk–Return Relationship

Try answering the questions developed by Michael Lipper, president of Lipper Analytical Services in New York. Lipper's questionnaire is one of the best around because it puts a clear focus on the risk–return relationship.

Get out a pen and paper or scribble in the margins of this book and try out the risk test. If you score 5, you have a low tolerance for risk. A score of 10 means you're a moderate investor, while a score of 25 designates you as a risk taker. Circle your answers and add up the numbers.

- My investment is for the long term. The end result is more important than how I went about achieving it.
  1. Totally disagree;
  2. Can accept variability, but not losses of capital;
  3. Can accept reasonable amounts of price fluctuation in total return;
  4. Can accept an occasional year of negative performance in the interest building capital;
  5. Agree.
- Rank the importance of current income.
  1. Essential and must be known;
  2. Essential but willing to accept uncertainty about the amount;
  3. Important, but there are other factors to consider;
  4. Modest current income is desirable;
  5. Irrelevant.
- Rank the amount of decline you can accept in a single quarter.
  1. None;
  2. A little, but not for the entire year;
  3. Consistency of results is more important than outperformance;
  4. A few quarters of decline is a small price to pay to be invested when the stock market takes off;
  5. Unimportant.
- Rank the importance of beating inflation.
  1. Preservation of capital and income are more important;

  2,3,4. Willing to invest to beat inflation, but other investment needs come first;

  5. Essential to insure that you get a real return on your investment.

- Rank the importance of beating the stock market over the economic cycle.
  1. Irrelevant;
  2,3,4. Prefer consistency over superior results;
  5. Critical.

Splitting Up the Mutual Fund Pie

Once you've evaluated your level of risk, you are ready to divide up your mutual fund portfolio among U.S. and overseas stock and bond funds. To make it easy for you to get the right investment mix, I have used CDA Technologies asset mix software to list the right investment percentages. The appropriate risk levels run low (10) to high (80) for most investors. So assess your risk tolerance level and look at the suggested percentage breakdown of investments.

As you can see from Tables 11–1 and 11–2, the more risk you are willing to take, the less money you put in money funds and the more you invest in stock funds. As you reach for return, you put more into overseas stock funds and aggressive U.S. equity funds. Foreign bond funds and money funds act to reduce risk, and precious metals give you an inflation hedge.

Table 11–1
Your Mix
(Levels are low risk to high risk)

Level	*Foreign Bond Fund (%)*	*Growth & Income Funds (%)*	*International Stock Funds (%)*	*Precious Metals Funds (%)*	*Money Funds (%)*	*Aggressive Growth Funds (%)*
10	7.5	0.5	1.0	2.0	81.5	7.5
20	6.5	1.0	7	3.5	72	10
30	5.5	10.0	11.0	5.0	60	8.5
40	5.0	6.0	15	6.0	53	15
50	5.0	6.5	19.5	7.5	44.5	17
60	5.0	5.5	24	8.5	34	23
70	5.0	7.0	26	10	25	27
80	3.5	10.0	32.5	11.5	14.5	28

Source: CDA Technologies.

Table 11–2
Your Mix—Expected Return and Range

Level	*Expected Return (%)*	*Standard Deviation (%)*
10	9.0	3.0
20	9.6	4.1
30	10.3	5.6
40	10.8	7.1
50	11.4	8.8
60	12.0	10.5
70	12.5	12.2
80	13.2	14.4

Source: CDA Technologies.

Table 11–1 shows you your risk tolerance and the right mix. Table 11–2 shows you the range of returns you can expect to make over the next 12 months.

The expected return is a mathematical forecast that says you have a 50-50 chance of earning. If you are a moderate risk investor, you could earn about 10.2 percent from a mutual fund portfolio split 5.5 percent in foreign bond funds, 10 percent in U.S. growth and income funds, 11 percent in overseas stock funds, 5 percent in precious metals funds, 60 percent in money funds, and 8.5 percent in aggressive U.S. stock funds.

The standard deviation (*SD*) of the return essentially represents the range of returns you can expect about 68 percent of the time. It's the margin of error or price swing. The *SD* is an indication of volatility. So this mix has an expected return of 10.2 percent with a standard deviation of 5.6 percent. That means you run about a 68 percent chance of making between 4.6 and 15.8 percent over the following year.

Say you want more growth. You could expect to earn 12 percent over the next year by using the following mix of assets: 5 percent in foreign bond funds, 5.5 percent in growth and income funds, 24 percent in overseas stock funds, 8.5

percent in precious metals funds, 34 percent in a money fund, and 23 percent in an aggressive stock fund.

This mix would have a price swing of 10.5 percent. So you run about a 68 percent chance of making between 2.5 percent and 22.5 percent.

Look at your risk tolerance. Then match it with the level of risk listed in Table 11–1. This will give you the right mix of assets based on your investment comfort level.

REVIEW YOUR INVESTMENTS

After you set your mix of assets, review the value of each asset and your total assets every six months to a year. You will find that some assets have grown, whereas others have declined in value. You have to rebalance the portfolio to keep the same mix of assets. When you rebalance, you take profits in winning assets and buy more shares in the assets that have declined in value. This is dollar cost averaging. When you buy more at a lower price, you get profits when the asset rebounds. Then you take profits, for example, in bonds and invest in stocks.

→ ACTION ITEM ←

Review your financial condition, goals, and tolerance for risk. If conditions change, you may have to redivide your investment pie more frequently than once or twice a year.

CONCLUSION

Split up your mutual fund investments. You can't go wrong. If you want some growth, but are afraid of losing too much money in the stock market, you would keep most of your money in bonds and money funds. The more growth or long-term gains you want, the more you weigh your variable insurance investments in stock market mutual funds.

POINTS TO REMEMBER

- When you purchase a variable life insurance policy or annuity, you can invest in common stock and bond mutual funds. These investments may pay higher returns than fixed rate whole life insurance products, but the market value of the mutual funds can drop due to economic conditions.
- Mutual funds are professionally managed and diversified portfolios of stocks or bonds. Mutual funds are considered a less risky investment compared with individual securities.
- Stocks have historically grown at an annual rate of 10 percent over the past 60 years. Over the short term, however, you can lose 10 percent or more in a common stock mutual fund.
- Bonds have grown at a 5 percent annual rate over the past 60 years. Over the short term, however, you can lose more than 5 percent in a bond mutual fund.
- Ask yourself how much risk you are willing to assume when you invest in mutual funds. If you are not willing to experience short-term losses in return for long-term gains, then you are better off buying a whole life insurance that pays a fixed rate of return.
- Diversification reduces risk because stocks, bonds, and money fund returns don't generally move in tandem. Gains in one asset can offset losses in other assets.
- A 50-50 stock and bond investment mix has grown at a 7.5 percent annual rate over the past 60 years. You earn 75 percent of the return on a 100 percent stake in the stock market, with half the risk of losing money.
- Review your portfolio and tolerance for risk at least twice a year.

12

How You or Your Beneficiaries Get Paid

Several settlement options are used to distribute death benefits or annuity proceeds. The payout options range from lump-sum payments to monthly income checks for life.

CASH SETTLEMENT

When you select the cash settlement option for an annuity or life insurance policy, your beneficiary receives a lump-sum distribution from the insurance company. Neither the life insurance policyholder nor the beneficiary is subject to income tax on the proceeds. If your estate is worth more than $600,000, the death benefits may be subject to estate taxes.

If you have an annuity, you have the same choice of settlement options as with life insurance. But you will pay taxes on the earnings in the annuity. You don't pay taxes on the principal. Ask your financial planner or agent about the tax consequences before you decide on an annuity settlement option. Your financial advisor can calculate the taxable proportion of money in the annuity.

This option has several advantages and disadvantages. On the plus side, the beneficiary has immediate use of the funds.

If the person is a sophisticated investor or plans to hire a money manager, the payout can grow. On the minus side, the beneficiaries may not manage the money correctly. In addition, the cash settlement is subject to claims from the beneficiary's creditors. In most states, if the money remained with the insurance company, creditors would not have access to the money. They could, however, sue to get the income from the proceeds.

COLLECT JUST THE INTEREST

You can set up the policy so that your beneficiary will collect the interest income from the proceeds for life, but the principal will remain untouched. If you have the insurance company pay your heirs the interest income from the proceeds, you don't have to worry about low interest rates. Life insurers pay beneficiaries a guaranteed minimum interest rate of 4 to 4.5 percent. However, if the company's investment results are above what is guaranteed, it pays you the extra interest. You can also combine the interest-only option with other settlement options.

People who can't manage large sums of money may prefer the interest-only option. Beneficiaries collect worry-free income since the insurance company is managing the money. Your interest earnings grow tax deferred until you receive payouts.

If you choose this option, you must be sure that you are doing business with a financially sound insurance company. If the firm isn't top-rated by such nationally recognized firms as A.M. Best, Standard & Poor's, and Moody's, don't pick this option.

GET MONEY FOR A FIXED PERIOD

If you are unsure how you want to handle the proceeds to be distributed to your beneficiaries, you can select the fixed-period option. It is similar to the interest-only option because you insure your beneficiaries will collect any remaining balance of the insurance when you die.

You collect principal and interest for a specific time period. The longer the time frame of the payouts, the lower the payouts. The shorter the time frame, the larger the payouts.

WEALTH BUILDING PROFILE ***Wife to Receive High Payouts on Husband's Pension.*** Jacqueline, age 60, will receive $1,920 a month in income for 5 years on her husband's $100,000 policy assuming the insurance company pays her 6 percent interest, based on a 15-year period certain settlement option. After 5 years, she will begin receiving $860 a month during her lifetime. However, if she dies within 15 years, her children will inherit the remaining proceeds.

LIFE INCOME OPTION

The life income option enables your beneficiary to receive monthly income based on the beneficiary's life expectancy. You get high monthly payouts, but the insurance company keeps the remaining money in your account if he or she predeceases the payout life expectancy. Your family gets nothing. (See Table 12–1 to review how much money you get every month based on your settlement option.)

Table 12–1
Lifetime Payout Option on $100,000 at 6%

Age	*10 Year Certain*	*20 Year Certain*	*Life Only*	*Cash Refund*
50	$704	$686	$707	$697
80	791	743	804	781
70	931	797	989	928

Source: The New England.

For example, a person age 68 would collect approximately $1,750 a month from a $200,000 insurance policy. However, if the beneficiary died a year later, the insurance company would keep the remaining $179,000 in insurance money. The surviving family would not receive a penny.

LIFE INCOME WITH A CASH REFUND OR PERIOD CERTAIN

If the surviving spouse is willing to settle for less monthly income, he or she can leave the balance of the insurance money to his or her beneficiaries for a set period of 10 to 25 years. By law, insurance companies cannot hold onto insurance proceeds for more than 30 years.

This is known as the life income period certain option. It is the most widely used settlement option because the death benefit proceeds can be passed onto the heirs in the form of a cash refund or monthly payments.

WEALTH BUILDING PROFILE ***Heirs Get Balance of Insurance Benefits.*** Alice's husband Ralph died of a heart attack while they were on vacation. She's age 50. Their $300,000 whole life policy is set up so that she will collect income for a period of 20 years certain. She will continue to receive income for her lifetime after she reaches age 70. The insurance company guarantees she will collect $1,400 a month or $16,800 a year for as long as she lives.

Alice is in good health. She has a life expectancy of 35.5 years. So she is assured of $16,800 a year from the death benefits for a long time. However, if she dies unexpectedly in two years, her son Robert will receive the monthly check for 18 years.

The same 68-year-old beneficiary would receive about $1,636 a month with a life income option on a $200,000 policy. However, if the person died one year after payouts began, the children would receive payments the remaining 9 years of the 10-year period certain contract.

The advantages of the life income option with the period certain are that your money is professionally managed, your assets are protected from creditors, and the family will receive the remaining amount of the money when you die (see Table 12–1). Assuming you have $100,000 that earns 6 percent, you would collect $707 a month on a 10-year period certain contract if you started receiving the proceeds at age 50. If you began receiving the proceeds at age 60 or age 70, you would receive $804 and $989 a month respectively.

THE JOINT SURVIVOR AND LIFE INCOME OPTION

This option is used for retirement planning. It assumes that the cash value is paid out to support the husband and wife when they retire. After the death of the first spouse, the survivor may collect 2/3, 3/4, or 1/2 of the payouts for his or her lifetime. So, if a couple received $600 a month and one spouse died, the other spouse could collect $400 a month.

ACTION ITEM

If you can't decide how you want to invest the death benefit you are about to receive, many insurance companies will put the cash into a money fund for a short period of time. After you have recovered from the death of a loved one, you can make a clearheaded decision. You can invest the money in an annuity or mutual fund.

?

Can I change my settlement options? Can my beneficiaries?

You state in the contract how the proceeds should be distributed. The best time to make changes in settlement options is when you are alive. However, you can state in the contract that beneficiaries do have some flexibility in changing the settlement options.

Currently, I'm receiving interest income from death benefits. But I want to change how I'm paid. Can I do this?

A lot depends on your insurance company's rules and the contractual agreement. In many cases, you can withdraw funds or switch to an option that pays you monthly income of both principal and interest knowing that if you die, your heirs will collect the balance of the insurance money.

Instead of receiving a monthly check from the insurance company, can I have the insurance company reinvest the money and let my death benefit proceeds grow like a bank account?

There are rules about how long you can let money accumulate with the insurance company. Check with your insurance company because state laws differ. If you are a minor, however, the proceeds can be reinvested. Payouts will begin when you become an adult.

I'm about to retire. Can I use the cash value I've built up over the years in my whole life policy for retirement?

If you don't need the coverage, you can have the insurance company annuitize your cash values. Your insurance agent or financial planner would have the money invested in an immediate annuity that would pay you monthly income over your lifetime.

Once you begin receiving payments, you pay tax on the part of your income that represents interest earnings. You don't pay tax on the part that is considered principal. A 68-year-old who purchased a $60,000 immediate annuity could receive about $500 a month with a 10-year refund option. Taxes would be paid on about 45 percent of the income, or $225. Assuming the person was in the 28 percent tax bracket, federal income taxes on the payout would amount to $63.

Can I take my cash, invest in tax-free municipal bonds, and live off the interest income?

Talk to your financial planner before you make this move. If the money you take out is more than the premiums you paid, you would pay tax on the excess amount. In addition, to protect what you have, you have to diversify your investments and invest in the most creditworthy bond issuers. At today's rates, you can make between 5 and 6 percent in tax-free bond funds. That's equivalent to a taxable yield of 8.3 percent.

POINTS TO REMEMBER

- Talk with your financial planner about the ways your loved ones will receive the death benefits from your insurance policy. You have several options to pick from including a lump-sum cash payout or an annuity that distributes the proceeds over your lifetime.
- Financial planners advise many people to take proceeds in what is called a life with a period certain option. The

beneficiary receives payments for as long as he or she lives. But if the person dies, for example, within 20 years of receiving the first payment, the remaining balance of money would go to the heirs. Otherwise the insurance company would keep the remaining money.

- You choose a settlement option when you sign the life insurance contract. But you can change the option later on.
- If you take your death benefit proceeds in a lump sum, talk to your financial planner about how you should manage the money.
- The settlement options apply to both life insurance and annuities.

13

Creative Uses of Life Insurance

Financial planners say that many people are turning to life insurance for more than income protection in case the breadwinner dies. Many are structuring their insurance policies to take advantage of the policy loan provisions to provide them with a source of tax-free income years later in life. Others are using life insurance as a source of wealth replacement or to pay estate taxes.

BORROWING AGAINST THE CASH VALUE

Tapping your cash value is one of the most frequent uses of life insurance outside of protection. When unexpected bills start piling up or a child's college tuition payment is due, financial advisors often recommend families take out a low-cost loan from their life insurance.

Chapter 7 discusses how policyholders can borrow against 70 percent to 90 percent of the cash value built up in a life insurance policy. The cash value is the investment or savings portion of a life insurance policy. Part of the insurance payment or premiums buy death benefits and part of the money goes into an investment account that pays either fixed or variable rates of return. As a result, the cash value can be used as collateral for a low-interest loan that ranges from 6 percent to 8 or 9 percent.

In addition to lower borrowing rates, life insurance loans have two other attractive features that can't be matched by other lending institutions: The loan doesn't have to be repaid. Also, policyholders can choose to let the interest accrue as new debt, rather than pay it off annually. However, the death benefits are reduced by the amount of the outstanding loan when the policyholder dies. So if full insurance coverage is needed for the future, financial planners stress it's best to pay back the interest and principal on the loan.

AN EXTRA SOURCE OF RETIREMENT INCOME

You also can take advantage of the policy loan features and use universal life (UL) insurance as a source of retirement savings. Universal life enables you to make flexible premium payments. You can invest in a policy that pays a fixed rate or invest in a variable universal policy and put money in common stock and bond funds for greater capital appreciation.

People can get life insurance coverage and save for retirement with a universal life insurance policy (see Chapter 8). It can be a useful part of a retirement savings plan. You won't pay taxes on the policy loan. You do pay taxes on income from your IRA. If you have an annuity, you also pay income tax on that part of the annuity distribution representing earnings.

Here's how you set up a universal life insurance policy to give yourself tax-free retirement income.

Remember our policyholder in Chapter 8? A male, age 40, who was a nonsmoker, would make premium payments of $5,000 a year for 19 years and receive a $500,000 death benefit coverage. Assuming the cash value grew at a 7.5 percent internal rate of return—that's the return made, less fees, commissions, and other charges that are deducted from the policy—the money would grow to $220,715 by the time the 40-year-old was 60 years of age.

At age 60, the policyholder borrows $16,024 a year against the cash value over the next 35 years. So, at age 95, there's not much in the way of death benefits. Death benefits are reduced by the policy loans. But at age 80, the policyholder would still have a $215,000 death benefit.

Another variation of this tactic is to use universal life insurance as supplemental tax-free savings. There are limits as to how much you can put into a UL policy in a lump sum or over 7 years based on IRS rules. If you adhere to the rules, you can fund your UL policy to the legal limit and build cash fast tax-free. Several years later, you can borrow against the cash value free and clear of income tax.

For example, assume a UL policy stock fund earns 7.25 percent annually over the next two decades. A nonsmoking 44-year-old male could put $2,000 a year into the UL policy for 7 years for a total of $14,000. At age 65, the insured could take a $9,000 policy loan every year over the next three years for a total of $27,000.

YOU CREATE AN ESTATE

Retirees with excess cash they don't plan to spend can buy life insurance and pass on double or triple the original money tax-free to beneficiaries and avoid probate. To do that, some financial planners set up an insurance policy as a modified endowment contract. This type of contract is tricky. You modify an insurance policy by putting in more money than is required. As a result, if money is taken out of the policy prior to death via withdrawals or loans, the policy doesn't qualify as a life insurance contract according to IRS rules. Hence, it is called a modified endowment contract.

Here is how it works: You overfund a life insurance contract and set up what is called a modified endowment contract, advises James Ludwick, an agent with Prudential Insurance Company, Tampa, FL. For example, someone who put $50,000 into a variable life policy and bought a $100,000 death benefit would double his or her money. When the insured dies, the beneficiaries would collect $150,000 tax-free.

Ludwick cautions, however, that you can't borrow against the cash value of a modified endowment contract unless you are willing to pay income taxes on the withdrawal. In addition, you must be careful that the insurance proceeds do not trigger estate taxes upon death of the insured.

AVOIDING THE PENSION TRAP

You don't necessarily have to take a drastic cut in your pension payout if you want continued income for your surviving spouse. Yet, many employees about to retire or forced into early retirement are grappling with which routes to take.

The Federal Employee Retirement Income Security Act (FICA) provides two options to most married employees who are entitled to a pension from their employer. Option A provides a lifetime pension for the retired employee, but if the employee dies before his or her spouse, no lifetime pension is payable to the surviving spouse. This is known as the maximum pension or life only payout option.

By contrast, Option B, the joint and survivor option, provides a reduced lifetime pension of about 20 percent for the retired employee. If the employee dies first, 50 to 75 percent of the monthly income is continued to the surviving spouse.

Most people want to be sure their spouse will have a monthly income. As a result, many take the lower payment through the joint and survivor payout options. But there are other ways to maximize your retirement income and avoid the pension squeeze. An employee could choose the maximum pension and purchase a cash value policy that will provide death benefits to the surviving spouse. The proceeds from the policy would pay as much as the surviving spouse would receive from the joint pension payout.

Pension maximization can work this way. A 53-year-old employee plans to retire in about 10 years. At age 65, he or she can draw $3,000 a month from the pension by using the maximum payout option. If the joint pension payout is selected, the retiree gets $2,400 a month. The spouse will receive $1,200 a month for his or her lifetime when the breadwinner dies.

The employee, however, can choose the higher pension payout of $3,000. He would then take some of the excess difference between the full payout and his joint and survivor payout of $600 and purchase a cash value life insurance policy. In this case, the employee would pay a monthly premium of approximately $408 a month over 12 years for $170,000 of life insurance to replace the wealth that's lost when the breadwinner dies and the pension money stops coming in.

When the employee retires or is forced to retire, he or she would receive a $3,000 a month pension instead of $2,400 and get an extra $600 of income each month. When the retiree dies, the surviving spouse gets $170,000 death benefits. The death benefit proceeds, if annuitized generate $1,200 monthly over the spouse's lifetime.

Despite the appeal of using life insurance for pension wealth replacement, it's not for everyone.

For example, some illustrations may overestimate the cash buildup. This can be troublesome. The reason: Many employees are sold vanishing premium policies. Premiums are paid for 10 to 12 years and the policy is paid up. But if interest rates move lower and the insurance company is forced to pay lower dividends or interest, you may have to pay more for your life insurance coverage. For every 1 percent drop in interest rates, policyholders might have to kick in an extra 2 years of premium payments. That could amount to paying several more thousand dollars to keep the insurance policy in force. The cost of buying an insurance policy may then be too expensive for pension maximization to work.

Other drawbacks include:

- If you are in poor health, you will not qualify for life insurance coverage.
- The cost of insurance for those over 65 years of age could be prohibitive. It works best with younger employees.

"Replacing a joint and survivor benefit with insurance can be effective for those age 60 or less," says Brad Fowler, actuary with Milliman & Robertson, Inc., Seattle, WA. "But beginning at age 65, life insurance starts to get pretty expensive."

Fowler adds that pension maximization will not work if the pension plan has a cost-of-living adjustment. It may be too expensive to purchase a whole life policy that will keep pace with the pension payment increases.

However, experts agree that pension maximization can work under a combination of two conditions: The pension has a low payout and insurance can be purchased at a reasonable cost.

Cost savings come from buying insurance illustrated at or close to the insurance company's guaranteed rate of 4.5 percent. That way, you avoid having to kick in extra premiums because the insurance agent overestimated the accumulated value of your life insurance policy's worth.

William Payne, a CLU, ChFC financial planner with PRW Associates, Inc., Braintree, MA (suburban Boston), says you have to explore all the options before you purchase life insurance—other sources of income, life insurance, personal savings, and the level pension benefit payouts.

"The employee has to look at providing additional cash flow in retirement," says Payne. "If an employee plans in advance for retirement, it can be done. But when the annual cost of paying life insurance premiums is more than the annual cost savings between the employee taking the maximum pension and the joint pension, wealth replacement with life insurance does not work."

Payne cites the case of an employee age 62 with a spouse age 62. That employee could not use life insurance to maximize the payout. The cost of the insurance is too expensive. Under the maximum payout, the employee receives $2,461 a month. He would get just $211 less a month or $2,532 a year from the joint and survivor option. The spouse receives $1,485 from the joint and survivor payout when the breadwinner dies.

However, the employee must pay premiums of $333 a month or $4,000 a year to buy enough insurance to fund $1,485 of income for the surviving spouse.

What happens if the spouse predeceases the retiree? An employee that selected the joint and survivor payout would lose benefits if he outlived the other spouse.

If there is any doubt about the health of the other spouse, Payne suggests taking a lump sum payment from the pension plan and transferring the money into an IRA. The money must be paid out over the joint life expectancy of the couple when the employee reaches age 70½. As a result, the payouts are much higher compared with payments from the pension plan or insurance annuity. And when the second spouse dies, the IRA money goes to the beneficiaries. By contrast, the beneficiaries would not inherit the money in the pension plan.

Although IRA payouts must draw the savings down to a zero balance based on life expectancy, Payne adds that it is rare for the funds to be depleted. To prevent such an occurrence, he suggests that the retiree reinvest part of the IRA proceeds.

ESTATE TAX PLANNING

Life insurance is also being used to pay huge estate tax bills.

Individuals with estates worth more than $600,000 are using life insurance for wealth replacement. Life insurance proceeds are either being used to pay the estate tax bill upon death or as wealth replacement to make up for the shortfall caused by paying federal and state estate taxes.

Second-to-die insurance is often used for estate planning. The policy insures two people and pays only on the second death. Estates are passed on tax-free to the surviving spouse under the marital deduction. When the second spouse dies, estate taxes are due. The second-to-die policy will pay the estate taxes due when the surviving spouse passes away.

Here is how a second-to-die policy can save you money. Couple A has no plan for their $2 million estate. Money is passed onto the surviving spouse free and clear of estate taxes. But when the second spouse dies, estate taxes of $600,000 are due and the heirs will receive $1.4 million.

By contrast, couple B takes steps to avoid the hefty estate tax bill. At age 40, the couple would set up an irrevocable insurance trust. Assets in an irrevocable trust are not considered to be part of a taxable estate. The couple would pay an annual premium of $5,820 and fund the trust with a $600,000 second-to-die insurance policy. The $600,000 benefit, which is available from day one, will pay the estate taxes. Couple B will be able to pass the entire $2 million to their heirs.

IMMEDIATE ANNUITIES FOR EXTRA INCOME

People living on a fixed income know all about interest rate risk. Every year or two, they are faced with rolling over their CDs at lower and lower interest rates.

Immediate annuities may be a solution to the CD rollover problem. The big advantage of immediate annuities over CDs: You know you'll get a monthly check from your annuity for as long as you live. In addition, you can pass on proceeds to your loved ones when you die. With one of the most common contracts, called "10 year certain and life," monthly checks keep coming for a minimum of 10 years. If the annuitant dies before the 10-year period is up, the checks are sent to a designated beneficiary until the 10 years are up. You can also set up the payout so your loved ones get a check for 15 or 20 years.

Remember that with an annuity, part of your money is considered a return of principal and the other part is considered taxable earnings. You give your money to the insurance company. The insurance companies then base the payout amount on the number of people who buy their annuity product, the annuitants' life expectancy, and the earnings on the company's investment portfolio.

For that reason, you can't directly compare an annuity with a CD which is a debt obligation. When a CD matures, you get all your principal back. You are free to reinvest the money as you like. It's your money.

There are other advantages to investing in immediate annuities if you are a safety conscious saver. For example:

- *Tax advantages.* You only pay taxes on part of the monthly income you receive from an annuity. Depending on your contract, you would pay taxes on about 30 to 40 percent of your monthly check. For example, if you receive $400 a month from your annuity, you pay the taxman on $130. Assuming you are in the 28 percent tax bracket, you owe Uncle Sam about $36 a month.
- *Favorable monthly income compared to CDs.* Today's payouts from some of the strongest insurance companies stack up favorably against CDs.

For example, assume a 70-year-old widow locked $50,000 into a 5 percent, 5-year CD at the local bank. She would earn $2,500 in interest income from the CD. Assuming she is in the 28 percent tax bracket, she earns $1,800 in after-tax income.

By contrast, if she bought a $50,000 immediate annuity with a 10-year certain and life from a financially sound insurance company, she would get a check for about $385 a month or $4,620 a year for as long as she lives.

The taxable part of her monthly annuity income is $143 and she owes Uncle Sam $40 a month. After taxes, she earns $103 from the annuity investment earnings or $1,236 a year. The total after-tax income, which includes principal and interest income, is $345 a month or $4,140 a year.

You get less after-tax income from the taxable portion of the annuity compared to the income from a 5-year CD. However, you get the annuity income for a lifetime. By contrast, you may not earn the same interest income from the 5 percent CD when it matures in 1998. You might roll the money over at more or less than 5 percent depending on what rates are five years from now. And if you took principal from your

CD comparable to an immediate annuity payment, you would deplete your funds in just a few years.

There is no free lunch, however, with an immediate annuity. There are several drawbacks to the product.

- Since you've already put the money in and signed the contract, you can't surrender an immediate annuity contract.
- You earn a net rate of return on your annuity. The insurance company earns a spread on what they pay you and what they earn on their investments that can amount to 2 to 3 percent.
- There are only a fistful of large and financially sound insurance companies that sell immediate annuities. New York Life Insurance Company, Guardian Life Insurance Company, Northwestern Mutual Life Insurance Company, and State Farm Life Insurance Company are all rated A++ by A.M. Best and carry triple A claims-paying ratings by at least one of the rating agencies.
- Insurance companies may change their payout rates for new contracts depending on the current level of interest rates.
- If an insurance company goes bankrupt, you may not get all of your money back. By contrast, your CDs are federally insured for $100,000 in the event a bank or thrift fails.
- Depending on where you live, you may pay a state premium tax on your annuity.

What can you expect to earn today from an immediate annuity? If you are interested in an immediate annuity, shop around. The amount of monthly income you receive can vary as much as $60 a month by company on a $100,000 annuity. On average, based on currently available data, a male or a female age 70 could expect to receive about $850 a month and $790 a month, respectively, on a $100,000 10-year certain and life plan.

Glossary

accidental death benefit A benefit in addition to the face amount of a life insurance policy, payable if the insured dies as the result of an accident (sometimes referred to as "double indemnity").

actuary Someone professionally trained in the technical aspects of insurance and related fields, particularly in the mathematics of insurance (the calculation of premiums, reserves, and other values).

adjustable life insurance A type of insurance that allows the policyholder to change the plan of insurance, raise or lower the face amount of the policy, increase or decrease the premium, and lengthen or shorten the protection period.

agent A sales and service representative of an insurance company. Life insurance agents may also be called life underwriters or field underwriters.

annuitant The person during whose life an annuity is payable, usually the person to receive the annuity.

This glossary is reprinted with permission of The American Council of Life Insurance.

annuity A contract that provides a periodic income at regular intervals for a specified period of time, such as for a number of years or for life.

annuity certain A contract that provides an income for a specified number of years, regardless of life or death.

annuity consideration The payment, or one of the regular periodic payments, an annuitant makes for an annuity.

application A statement of information made by someone applying for life insurance. The information gathered helps the life insurance company assess the acceptability of risk.

assignment The legal transfer of one person's interest in an insurance policy to another person.

automatic premium loan A provision in a life insurance policy that any premium not paid by the end of the grace period (usually 31 days) is automatically paid by a policy loan if there is sufficient cash value.

beneficiary The person named in the policy to receive the insurance proceeds at the death of the insured.

broker A sales and service representative who handles insurance for clients, generally selling insurance of various kinds and/or several companies.

business life insurance Life insurance purchased by a business enterprise on the life of a member of the firm. It is often bought by partnerships to protect the surviving partners against loss caused by the death of a partner, or by a corporation to reimburse it for loss caused by the death of a key employee (also known as *key person insurance*).

cash surrender value The amount available in cash upon voluntary termination of a policy by its owner before it becomes payable by death or maturity.

certificate A statement issued to individuals insured under a group policy, setting forth the essential provisions relating to their coverage.

certified financial planner (CFP) A designation awarded to those specializing in all aspects of financial planning.

certified public accountant (CPA) Accountants who pass a national exam, but are licensed by the state. A CPA with a designation of Accredited Personal Financial Planning Specialist (APFS) has passed a national exam on all aspects of financial planning.

chartered financial analyst (CFA) A designation for those specializing in the securities analysis.

chartered financial consultant (ChFC) A designation awarded to those specializing in financial planning.

chartered life underwriter (CLU) A designation awarded to those specializing in all aspects of life insurance.

chartered property casualty underwriter (CPCU) A designation awarded to those specializing in property and casualty insurance.

claim Notification to an insurance company that payment of an amount is due under the terms of the policy.

convertible term insurance Term insurance that can be exchanged, at the option of the policyholder and without evidence of insurability, for another plan of insurance.

cost index A way to compare the costs of similar plans of life insurance. A policy with a smaller index number is generally a better buy than a comparable policy with a larger index number.

cost-of-living rider An option that permits the policyholder to purchase increasing term insurance coverage. The death proceeds increase by a stated amount each year, to coincide with an estimated increase in the cost of living.

credit life insurance Term life insurance issued through a lender or lending agency to cover payment of a loan, installment purchase or other obligation, in case of death.

declination The rejection by a life insurance company of an application for life insurance, usually for reasons of health or occupation.

deferred annuity An annuity providing for the income payments to begin at some future date.

deferred group annuity A type of group annuity providing for the purchase each year of a paid-up deferred annuity for each member of the group, the total amount received by the member at retirement being the sum of these deferred annuities.

deposit administration group annuity A type of group annuity providing for the accumulation of contributions in an undivided fund out of which annuities are purchased as the members of the group retire.

deposit term insurance A form of term insurance, not really involving a "deposit," in which the first-year premium is larger than subsequent premiums. Typically, a partial endowment is paid at the end of the term period. In many cases, the partial endowment can be applied toward the purchase of a new term policy or, perhaps, a whole life policy.

disability benefit A feature added to some life insurance policies providing for waiver of premium, and sometimes payment of monthly income, if the policyholder becomes totally and permanently disabled.

dividend A return of part of the premium on participating insurance to reflect the difference between the premium charged and the combination of actual mortality, expense, and investment experience. Such premiums are calculated to provide some margin over the anticipated cost of the insurance protection.

dividend addition An amount of paid-up insurance purchased with a policy dividend and added to the face amount of the policy.

endowment Life insurance payable to the policyholder if living, on the maturity date stated in the policy, or to a beneficiary if the insured dies prior to that date.

expectation of life *see* life expectancy.

extended term insurance A form of insurance available as a nonforfeiture option. It provides the original amount of insurance for a limited period of time.

face amount The amount stated on the face of the insurance policy that will be paid in case of death or at the maturity of the policy. It does not include additional amounts payable under accidental death or other special provisions, or acquired through the application of policy dividends.

family policy A life insurance policy providing insurance on all or several family members in one contract, generally whole life insurance on the principal breadwinner and small amounts of term insurance on the spouse and children, including those born after the policy is issued.

flexible premium policy or annuity A life insurance policy or annuity under which the policyholder or contract holder may vary the amounts or timing of premium payments.

flexible premium variable life insurance A life insurance policy that combines the premium flexibility feature of universal life insurance with the equity-based benefit feature of variable life insurance.

fraternal life insurance Life insurance provided by fraternal orders or societies to their members.

grace period A period (usually 30 or 31 days) following the premium due date, during which an overdue premium may be paid without penalty. The policy remains in force throughout this period.

group annuity A pension plan providing annuities at retirement to a group of people under a master contract. It is usually issued to an employer for the benefit of employees. The individual members of the group hold certificates as evidence of their annuities.

group life insurance Life insurance usually without medical examination, on a group of people under a master policy. It is typically issued to an employer for the benefit of employees, or to members of an association, for example, a professional membership group. The individual members of the group hold certificates as evidence of their insurance.

guaranteed insurability An option that permits the policyholder to buy additional stated amounts of life insurance at stated times in the future without evidence of insurability.

individual policy pension trust A type of pension plan, frequently used for small groups, administered by trustees who are authorized to purchase individual level premium policies or annuity contracts for each member of the plan. The policies usually provide both life insurance and retirement benefits.

industrial life insurance Life insurance issued in small amounts, usually less than $1,000, with premiums payable on a weekly or monthly basis. The premiums are generally collected at the home by an agent of the company. Sometimes referred to as debit insurance.

insurability Acceptability to the company of an applicant for insurance.

insurance examiner The representative of a state insurance department assigned to participate in the official audit and examination of the affairs of an insurance company.

insured or insurer life The person on whose life the policy is issued.

lapsed policy A policy terminated for nonpayment of premiums. The term is sometimes limited to a termination occurring before the policy has a cash or other surrender value.

legal reserve life insurance company A life insurance company operating under state insurance laws specifying the minimum basis for the reserves the company must maintain on its policies.

level-premium life insurance Life insurance for which the premium remains the same from year to year. The premium is more than the actual cost of protection during the earlier years of the policy and less than the actual cost in the later years. The building of a reserve is a natural result of level premiums. The overpayments in the early years, together with the interest that is to be earned, serve to balance out the underpayments of the later years.

life annuity A contract that provides an income for life.

life expectancy The average number of years of life remaining for a group of persons at a given age according to a particular mortality table.

life insurance in force The sum of the face amounts, plus dividend additions, of life insurance policies outstanding at a given time. Additional amounts payable under accidental death or other special provisions are not included.

limited payment life insurance Whole life insurance on which premiums are payable for a specified number of years or until death, if death occurs before the end of the specified period.

master policy A policy that is issued to an employer or trustee, establishing a group insurance plan for designated members of an eligible group.

mortality table A statistical table showing the death rate at each age, usually expressed as so many per thousand.

mutual fund A diversified and professionally managed portfolio of securities that may include stocks or bonds. Policyholders have a choice of investing their cash values in stock or bond mutual funds when they own a variable or universal variable life insurance product.

mutual life insurance company A life insurance company without stockholders whose management is directed by a board elected by the policyholders. Mutual companies, in general, issue participating insurance.

nonforfeiture option One of the choices available if the policyholder discontinues premium payments on a policy with a cash value. This, if any, may be taken in cash, as extended term insurance or as reduced paid-up insurance.

nonforfeiture values The value, if any, either in cash or in another form of insurance, available upon failure to make the required premium payments.

nonmedical limit The maximum face value of a policy that a given company will issue without the applicant taking a medical examination.

nonparticipating insurance Insurance on which no dividends are paid.

nonparticipating policy A life insurance policy in which the company does not distribute to policyholders any part of its surplus. Premiums for nonparticipating policies are usually lower than for comparable participating policies. Also, some nonparticipating policies have both a maximum premium and a current lower premium. The current premium reflects anticipated experience that is more favorable than the company is willing to guarantee, and it may be changed from time to time for the entire block of business to which the policy belongs. *See also* participating policy.

ordinary life insurance Life insurance usually issued in amounts of $1,000 or more with premiums payable on an annual, semiannual, quarterly, or monthly basis.

paid-up insurance Insurance on which all required premiums have been paid. The term is frequently used to mean the reduced paid-up insurance available as a nonforfeiture option.

participating policy A life insurance policy under which the company agrees to distribute to policyholders the part of its surplus which its board of directors determines is not needed at the end of the business year. Such a distribution serves to reduce the premium the policyholder has paid. *See also* policy dividend; nonparticipating policy.

permanent life insurance A phrase used to cover any form of life insurance except term; generally insurance that accrues cash value, such as whole life or endowment.

policy The printed legal document stating the terms of the insurance contract that is issued to the policyholder by the company.

policy dividend A refund of part of the premium on a participating life insurance policy reflecting the difference between the premium charged and actual experience.

policy loan A loan made by a life insurance company from its general funds to a policyholder on the security of the cash value of a policy.

policy reserves The measure of the funds that a life insurance company holds specifically for fulfillment of its policy obligations. Reserves are required by law to be calculated so that, together with future premium payments and anticipated interest earnings, they will enable the company to pay all future claims.

policyholder The person who owns a life insurance policy. This is usually the insured person, but it may also be a relative of the insured, a partnership, or a corporation.

premium The payment, or one of the periodic payments, a policyholder agrees to make for an insurance policy.

premium loan A policy loan made for the purpose of paying premiums.

rated policy Sometimes called an "extra-risk" policy, an insurance policy issued at a higher-than-standard premium rate to cover the extra risk where, for example, an insured has impaired health or a hazardous occupation.

reduced paid-up insurance A form of insurance available as a nonforfeiture option. It provides for continuation of the original insurance plan, but for a reduced amount.

reinstatement The restoration of a lapsed policy to full force and effect. The company requires evidence of insurability and payment of past due premiums plus interest.

renewable term insurance Term insurance that can be renewed the end of the term, at the option of the policyholder and without evidence of insurability, for a limited number of successive terms. The rates increase at each renewal as the insured grows older.

reserve The amount required to be carried as a liability in the financial statement of an insurer, to provide for future commitments under policies outstanding.

rider A special policy provision or group of provisions that may be added to a policy to expand or limit the benefits otherwise payable.

risk classification The process by which a company decides how its premium rates for life insurance should differ according to risk characteristics of individuals insured (e.g., age, occupation, sex, state of health) and then applies the resulting rules to individual applications. *See* underwriting.

separate account An asset account established by a life insurance company separate from other funds, used primarily for pension plans and variable life products. This arrangement permits wider latitude in the choice of investments, particularly in equities.

settlement options The several ways, other than immediate payment in cash, which a policyholder or beneficiary may choose to have policy benefits paid. *See also* supplementary contract.

stock life insurance company A life insurance company owned by stockholders who elect a board to direct the company's management. Stock companies, in general, issue nonparticipating insurance but may also issue participating insurance.

straight life insurance Whole life insurance on which premiums are payable for life.

supplementary contract An agreement between a life insurance company and a policyholder or beneficiary by which the company retains the cash sum payable under an insurance policy and makes payments in accordance with the settlement option chosen.

term insurance Life insurance payable to a beneficiary only when an insured dies within a specified period.

term rider Term insurance that is added to a whole life policy at the time of purchase or that may be added in the future.

underwriting The process by which a life insurance company determines whether it can accept an application for life insurance, and if so, on what basis.

universal life insurance A flexible premium life insurance policy under which the policyholder may change the death benefit from time to time (with satisfactory evidence of insurability for increases) and vary the amount or timing of premium payments. Premiums (less expense charges) are credited to a policy account from which mortality charges are deducted and to which interest is credited at rates that may change from time to time.

variable annuity An annuity contract in which the amount of each periodic income payment may fluctuate. The fluctuation may be related to securities market values, a cost-of-living index, or other variable factor.

variable life insurance Life insurance under which the benefits relate to the value of assets behind the contract at the time the benefit is paid. The amount of death benefit payable would, under variable life policies that have been proposed, never be less than the initial death benefit payable under the policy.

waiver of premium A provision that under certain conditions an insurance policy will be kept in full force by the company without further payment of premiums. It is used most often in the event of total and permanent disability.

whole life insurance Life insurance payable to beneficiary at the death of the insured, whenever that occurs. Premiums may be payable for a specified number of years (limited payment life), or for life (straight life).

Index

www.ingramcontent.com/pod-product-compliance
Lightning Source LLC
Chambersburg PA
CBHW030917180526
45163CB00002B/374

* 9 7 8 0 5 9 5 1 4 4 4 8 8 *